COMING TO CHRIST IN DEMENTIA

Mark Wormell

Copyright © 2015 Mark Wormell.

All rights reserved. Other than for the purposes of, and subject to the conditions prescribed under the Copyright Act, no part of this publication may be reproduced, stored in a retrieval system, or transmitted in any form or by any means, electronic, mechanical, photocopying, recording or otherwise without written permission from the publisher.

ISBN 978-0-9925595-2-6 (paperback)
ISBN 978-0-9925595-5-7 (e-book)

Contents

Contents 3
Introduction 8
Chapter 1
Some Preliminary Questions 14
    Why do Christians need to think about conversion in dementia? 14
    Does a diagnosis of dementia mean a person must now be left spiritually alone, and, as far as we know, have no hope of salvation? 16
    What ethical issues arise when sharing the gospel with people who have dementia? 17
    Isn't it all too hard? 17
    Are there helpful ways to understand how we learn and know things? 19
    Are there tools to help understand different ways of knowing? 20
    How does this understanding of knowledge help us? 21

Chapter 2
The Experience of Some Carers 23
    The questions I asked 23
    What changes did the carers observe? 25
    Does Bible reading help? 25
    Are verbal statements of faith common? 26
    If actions speak louder than words, do people change in character when they come to trust Jesus? 27

Is it ever too late? 27
What do carers need to do? 29
What ways of sharing the love and good news of Jesus seem to work best? 29
Are there any theological 'no-go areas'? 30
Do people with dementia approach time, and their experience of life in dementia, differently from the way others approach time and life? 32
How can we know if someone has come to a new faith in Christ? 33

Chapter 3
The Effects of Dementia 36
Is there anything inherent in dementia that precludes the saving work of Jesus? 36
How does God reach someone with dementia, and will he show us how he does it? 37
If we are dependent, don't we need to know we are? 39
What is dementia? 39
What do we know about dementia? 40
What are some practical limitations of scientific knowledge? 41
What do we learn or come to remember in dementia? 42
How 'lost' are memories? 43
Conclusion 43

Chapter 4
Personhood, Self, Memory and Resurrection 45
Dementia poses questions to personhood, identity and faith 45
What are some unchristian perspectives on personhood? What are we fighting against? 46
How pervasive are these views? 47
If not 'capacity', how should we determine personhood? 47

What is the 'mind'? 48
Isn't the 'mind' like a computer? 49
What is a Christian perspective on personhood and knowing? 49
Who is a 'person' in God's eyes? 50
Don't we have bodies and souls? What if we lose our soul? 50
Aren't we what we think? 53
When my brain doesn't work as it used to, won't I lose my 'inner-self'? 54
Is science useless then? 55
Isn't losing our memories so like death that we might as well treat it as death? 55
What happens to our memories at death? 56
Aren't our memories important then? 58
Don't we need our brains to experience God? 58
How does dementia affect our reception of God's grace? 59
What does the Bible say about knowing God in dementia? 59
How might God see our knowing? 60
Why might we think that God will save people with dementia? 61
How can a person with dementia know God if he/she does not recognise people he/she once knew and loved, e.g. a spouse or child? 62
Conclusion 62

Chapter 5
Salvation by Grace 63
What do we need to do/be/think/believe to be saved? 63
What does it mean to have faith? 64
Are God's words still important? 65
Are we changing the doctrine of justification by faith? 67
What does *faith* looks like when control of thought

and speech are diminished? 67
How may someone with dementia express faith? 68
Should not faith be shown in works? 69
Faith is about a relationship. How can someone with dementia have a relationship with God when they sometimes don't appear to relate to their immediate family or anyone else? 69
How does dementia affect the sense that there is a God or divine power? 70
Surely we have to do something to find God? Isn't that 'something' beyond someone with dementia? 71
Doesn't faith in God include rejecting things that are wrong, like false gods? How does this work for someone with dementia? 72
If someone with dementia can believe, can they truly repent? 72
If someone with dementia can believe and repent, can they persevere? 74
What about anti-social behaviour and 'sin' in dementia? 75
Does it help to think that 'sins' in dementia are unintentional? 75
Is there a time in advanced dementia when we cannot reasonably expect any change in that person's relationship with God? 76
Conclusion 77

Chapter 6
Christian Care that Supports God's Work of Salvation 78
Identity 78
Can we really talk of 'evangelism' to people with dementia? 81
Is special training required? 82
Do we really want to use the 'evangelism' word? 83
What should we do when non-Christian children try to stop their parent in a facility from attending

>   chapel or discussing religious subjects? 84
> Won't the binary nature of salvation/damnation
>   scare or upset vulnerable people who can't
>   handle these challenges? 84
> If we speak of the love of Jesus, won't they just
>   forget? 85
> What outside pressures restrict this work? 85
> What can we do? 86

Conclusion 88
Acknowledgement and Thanks 90
Bibliography 91
>   Books cited 91
>   Articles cited 95

Introduction

Recently my father died with cognitive-dementia. He was a brilliant man, working first as an aeronautical engineer for over 45 years and then collecting his PhD in classics at the age of 77. However, within a few years, he could not count backwards in 3s. My father-in-law in Malaysia has dementia, and my bother-in-law has retired and left his home in North Queensland to go and care for his father. A number of my uncles and aunts have dementia. A cousin has early onset dementia. My sister is a nurse who has worked with people with dementia for over 30 years.

As a parish pastor I talk with many people who care for family and friends who have a dementia diagnosis.[1] They have many questions about dementia and faith. They worry about whether they are doing enough. They ask, can God be known by people who live with the effects of dementia? They need easier access to answers to the important questions they ask about how our Heavenly Father loves and protects people with dementia.

Through my work and through my family I have become more aware of the special needs of people who have dementia, and also the great challenges in caring for them well.

---

1 'Having a dementia diagnosis', is the position on language and labelling preferred by Alzheimer's Australia. Some providers of dementia care prefer to use, 'living with dementia'.

Some of the questions people ask are relational. How do we show our love to people with dementia? How do we show God's love to people with dementia? Some of these challenges are ethical and take on a particular shape when the care is provided by a Christian organisation or church. When should carers[2] intervene when a person with dementia is behaving outside the way they behaved before or in a sinful manner? To what extent should carers listen to instructions from the children or guardians of people with dementia when those instructions appear motivated by self-interest or ignorance or antagonism to faith?

For some, the questions are even more basic. What is dementia and what will it do to me or the person I love?[3]

When I started researching these issues there appeared to be a gap in the literature on Christian care for people who enter dementia without a saving faith. There are good books on care for Christians who get dementia. A number of theologians have addressed God's work in dementia, but usually in the context of what dementia means for a Christian.[4] Stephen Post has observed: 'The emergence of Spirituality in AD [Alzheimer's Disease] has not yet been examined, but it may be worth a study'.[5] That study appears to have not been published yet. We will see that John Swinton has done some outstanding work evaluating

---

[2] I will use the word 'carer' to include all people who provide care. These include family members, friends, people from local churches, pastoral workers and chaplains.

[3] I give a definition of dementia at p.39, However, with others who work in this field, I think it is better to not focus too quickly on the medical nature and consequences of dementia, as that can cloud our appreciation of the ongoing humanity of the people we seek to care for. First we need to see them as God sees them, so we do not start by seeing them as 'patients' or 'sufferers' or less than fully human.

[4] For example, Swinton, *Dementia*, David Keck, *Forgetting Whose We Are: Alzheimer's Disease and the Love of God*, (Nashville, Tenn: 1996) and Stephen G. Post, *The Moral Challenge of Alzheimer Disease: Ethical Issues from Diagnosis to Dying*, Second Edition (Baltimore: John Hopkins Uni Press, 2000).

[5] Post, *Moral*, 138.

secular understandings of personhood, and dementia, from a Christian perspective, and putting forward a biblically convincing Christian view of personhood and memory. He offers great hope to those who enter dementia with faith, and his Christian anthropology opens the door for a theology of salvation in dementia.

Yet perhaps 80% of people around the world who are diagnosed with dementia are non-Christians.[6] It is curious that there are many books on understanding and caring for Christians with dementia, and none on how people become Christians in the midst of dementia.

This book is intended to begin to fill that gap. It is an aide for Christian carers, pastors, chaplains and others who are thinking about how their involvement with people with dementia may be used by God to bring people to faith in Jesus. I have great admiration for these people, and offer this book in humble service to them.

I also hope that theological colleges, and programs to train pastors, will ensure that their students and pastors have an adequate sense of the opportunities and significance of their work with people in dementia. There are many other books that need to be written to fill this gap. Only a few Christians have written of their experience of living with dementia,[7] and, as far as I am aware, no one has written on their experience of getting to know Jesus while living with dementia. I look forward to many books like that.

---

[6] Pew Research's Religion and Religious Life Project, and other agencies, put the percentage of Christians in the world at about 31.5%: see http://www.pewforum.org/2012/12/18/global-religious-landscape-exec/ accessed on 26/9/2013. However, the number of people with a lively personal faith in Jesus, perhaps evidenced by regular church attendance, is considerably less.

[7] For example, Robert Davis, an American Presbyterian pastor, chronicled his own experience of Alzheimer's disease, *My Journey into Alzheimer's Disease: Helpful Insights for Family and Friends* (Wheaton: Tyndall House, 1989).

In the meantime, we need to think about the questions asked by carers. For we worship a loving and sovereign God, who we can expect to meet us in our needs. We should expect him to express that love by saving people who enter dementia with no faith in Jesus, not because they have dementia, but because he is a God of love and power, who can save anyone he chooses. Furthermore, our hope can be more hopeful if our doubts about faith in dementia are reduced, and our care can be more directed if we understand better God's perspective on people with dementia.

Many people are more afraid of getting dementia than cancer. The behaviour of some with dementia suggests great fear and anxiety, yet we don't explore what the God who calms storms (Mark 4:35-41), tells us to not be afraid (Matthew 14:27) and brings peace (John 16:33), may be doing with people at the most frightening time of their lives. We need to break down those fears by considering the character and purposes of God, as he has revealed them to us.

The heart of the Gospel is that God sent his Son to be the saviour of the world. Christ accomplished this by dying an atoning death on the cross. The love embodied in these divine acts achieves its purpose when ordinary sinful people are led by the Holy Spirit to believe that Jesus did this for them, and thereby to trust their lives to Jesus, or, in other words, to have faith in Jesus (Romans 5:1-2; Galatians 3:15-16). They are, by no other act or knowledge, right with God. In this way they are justified by grace alone through faith. Being justified, we have no reason to fear the challenges of this world, including frailty, dementia and death, and the life to come.

One way to conquer these fears is to consider what this saving belief and trust looks like for someone who gets dementia.

As this book is, in part, a response to many questions I have heard asked by Christian carers and people whose loved ones have dementia, my approach will be to ask and propose answers to these questions. As many of the questions are theological, I will need to use theology to answer them. Some readers may be surprised by the directness, and baldness, of some questions, but I have heard them asked and we need to develop answers to them. If you have other questions, I would love to hear them.

I hope this 'question and answer' approach helps you dip in and dip out of this book, as not all questions may interest every reader.

A number of the questions spill out from a larger question: can people with dementia come to a saving trust in Christ? I will consider evidence that conversion does occur and philosophical and theological objections to conversion in dementia. However, I recognise this is a large and complex area that requires much more work. All I can do here is outline the issues and suggest some ways forward.

Besides addressing important, often heart-shattering, questions, I hope this book encourages Christian carers in their immeasurably valuable work in patient, persistent and loving care of people with dementia. There is so much cause for hope. I hope you see it. I also hope that this book resources pastoral care providers and challenges churches and Christians to present Jesus to people with a dementia diagnosis.

This hope comes in part from a number of interviews I conducted with people who care for people with dementia, particularly in the context of aged care facilities and palliative care. This research forms the core of this book. In chapter 1, I will consider some preliminary questions that help develop a framework for thinking about dementia and faith. In chapter 2, I look at evidence from these carers. In chapter 3, I explore questions about the nature and effect of dementia. In chapter 4, I consider the question posed by some atheist philosophers and some Christians: is there a person to save? In chapter 5, I address some of the key theological questions that emerge from our doctrine of salvation. In chapter 6, I ask what this means for the way we care for people with dementia, the way we participate in public discussions about aged care and the way we train our pastors.

Before I address these questions, I will comment briefly on the title of this book. It is a challenge to choose a title that is both short, and informative of content and approach. I thought of 'Salvation in Dementia', but was concerned that it may be thought that I may be suggesting that dementia was the means by which, rather than the context in which, salvation comes. 'Conversion in Dementia' may, for some, sound off-putting, or suggest too much human agency. A better, but longer title, may have been, 'Christ coming to us in Dementia', as the acts of revelation and transformation are always works of God. Nevertheless, 'Coming to Christ in Dementia' seems to fit well with Jesus' wonderful words of comfort in Matthew 11:28-30:

> *"Come to me, all you who are weary and burdened, and I will give you rest. Take my yoke upon you and learn from me, for I am gentle and humble in heart, and you will find rest for your souls. For my yoke is easy and my burden is light."*

Now it is time to address some preliminary questions.

Chapter 1

Some Preliminary Questions

Why do Christians need to think about conversion in dementia?

For some the word 'conversion' sounds harsh and they question why we need to discuss it at all. Correctly, they observe that conversion is always a mysterious act of God, and way beyond our comprehension. All we should want to do is provide the very best care we can, and leave the rest to God. I understand this approach. However, I do think we need to grapple with the question of conversion, for six reasons:

First, God usually uses Christians to bring his good news of love and salvation to people who do not know Him. Therefore, Christian carers need to be prepared for the practical and theological challenges they will face in sharing that good news with people who have dementia, just as we face these challenges with children, teenagers and seniors.

Second, while most older people who receive care do so at home,[1] many people with dementia in Australia (including early-onset dementia) are cared for in aged care facilities. These facilities are often run by Christian organisations, or employ Christians as chaplains and carers. Most of these

---

1 2014 Report on the Funding and Financing of the Aged Care Industry, https://www.dss.gov.au/our-responsibilities/ageing-and-aged-care/aged-care-reform/reforms-by-topic/aged-care-financing-authority/2014-report-on-the-funding-and-financing-of-the-aged-care-industry accessed on 11/08/2015.

organisations have committed and gifted people caring for people with dementia, and have worked out good ways to share the gospel with people with dementia. We can benefit from hearing the hopes they see, and their experiences.

Third, dementia is a large and growing problem. In Australia over 332,000 Australians live with it today,[2] and perhaps 46 million live with it worldwide.[3] Many more can be expected to get it as more people live beyond 85. Some have seen it as a 'western problem', but it is a growing problem in the developing world, as people live longer. In most developing countries there is very little specialist aged and dementia care.

Fourth, a debate has been running for several decades over whether people with dementia should be euthanised. This debate is escalating as the costs of aged care increase with the ageing population. Most Christians will oppose euthanasia on ethical grounds, but their opposition may gain sharper focus if they see new hope for eternal life while living with dementia.

Fifth, the question of government funding for dementia research and care for people with a dementia diagnosis is critical. As members of a democracy, many Christians in Australia would consider they have a biblical responsibility to advocate and vote in such a way that cares for people with a dementia diagnosis.

Sixth, the church both denominationally and locally/congregationally needs to wrestle with the priority it places on Christian ministry to people with a dementia diagnosis.

---

[2] Alzheimer's Australia has an excellent website with much practical advice and information. This statistic is taken from http://www.fightdementia.org.au/understanding-dementia/statistics.aspx, accessed on 28/7/2015.
[3] See https://www.alz.co.uk/research/WorldAlzheimerReport2015.pdf accessed on 12/12/2015.

Many churches are passionate to have scripture in the schools in their local area but have not considered ministry into local age care facilities or to people who are living in their community with a dementia diagnosis. Indeed, many are not investing much effort to care for people with a dementia diagnosis who are part of their church family.

Other reasons will become apparent below, but these are sufficient to get us started.

Does a diagnosis of dementia mean a person must now be left spiritually alone, and, as far as we know, have no hope of salvation?

This question can emerge from a desire to not upset people who have dementia, ignorance of dementia, or a sense that the effects of dementia limit access to the spiritual dimension of life. We need to overcome these barriers.

As will be discussed below, there are many different forms of dementia, and not all affect the way we think, our memories and the way we relate to each other. However, Alzheimer's disease is the most common, and does affect our memories and relationships, as do many other common forms of dementia. So the question becomes, can we engage with the spiritual needs of people with dementia?

The answer is clearly, 'yes'. First, there has been a growing emphasis on the spiritual needs of older people over the last 20-30 years.[4] Second, there is good evidence of conversion late into dementia, and good theological reasons to know that God can save until there is no longer the breath of life.

---

4 In Australia the well regarded work of Elizabeth MacKinlay has inspired many people to recognise and try to meet these needs. See, for example, *The Spiritual Dimension of Ageing*, (London: Jessica Kingsley Publishers, 2001) and with Corinne Trevitt, *Facilitating Spiritual Reminiscence for People with Dementia: A Learning Guide* (London: Jessica Kingsley Publishers, 2015).

Nevertheless, this is a challenging area. If someone has not accepted Christ in their youth, middle or old age, what hope or right has anyone to expect conversion as they live with dementia? We will see that God's grace provides compelling answers to these questions.

What ethical issues arise when sharing the gospel with people who have dementia?
For some, warning bells sound: don't go here! People with dementia are among the most vulnerable in society. There is no doubt the ethical issues are complex. All the carers I interviewed were acutely aware of the vulnerability and dependence of the people in their care, and the responsibility this placed on them as carers. However, as we will see, ignoring the spiritual is a form of 'de-personalisation' that has its own ethical challenges. Passions run hot in this area. Some Christian carers believe to not love people with a dementia diagnosis by sharing Jesus with them is a form of spiritual abuse.

Despite the challenges associated with engaging the spiritual needs of people with dementia, it could be said that much of the literature on Christian care and evangelism for the aged appears to have abandoned evangelism for those with dementia and thereby conceded the notions of 'loss of mind' and 'loss of person'. In doing so there is a risk of missing Christ's call to care for the vulnerable (Matthew 25:31-46) and to love our neighbour and God (Matthew 22:34-40).

Isn't it all too hard?
It certainly can be hard. At a practical level, the ease or difficulty will depend on a number of factors including the progression of the disease, the person's history, the help

available (it's harder if you are working alone), and the working of the Spirit. At a theological level, for some, there appears to be an implicit challenge to the core doctrine of justification by faith. We will need to consider what 'coming to faith' looks like for someone who appears to have compromised access to their memory, reflective thought and language. Many Christians appear to be ill equipped to deal with this, particularly if they hold that saving faith requires cognition, the very thing that dementia appears to attack.

I have heard people question whether to share the gospel with someone who has dementia is a waste of limited resources. They support care for the increasing physical and social needs of people with dementia, but ask if we should save the gospel for someone who can both comprehend and remember, and situations where the ethical challenges are less. This same argument is increasingly run with sharing the gospel with young children.

Quite a different story emerges when one speaks with Christians who care for people with dementia. At times, when doing my research, I was overwhelmed by the great stories of God's faithful work and love I heard. While in some cases it is difficult to read the signs of conversion (and that is not our role anyway!), these Christian carers provide very strong evidence that God saves people in dementia. The experience of these carers, and particularly their knowledge of the God who is powerful, listens to prayer and saves, leads them to think that God sees the smile and hears the brief muted 'thank you' or 'Amen' when someone with dementia responds to a hymn, prayer or embrace from a Christian carer. Their testimony is a powerful, varied and encouraging affirmation that God saves in dementia.

Some people suggest we do not need to consider these

questions because God is in control. He saves who he wants to save (John 13:18; Romans 8:29), and, if we don't always see or understand it, so be it. As mentioned above, conversion is always a work of God, so why not leave it to him, particularly given the ethical minefield?

Christians will have differing views on the gift of evangelism (1 Corinthians 12:8; Ephesians 4:11), and proclamation (1 Peter 2:11-12), and the effort God expects us to take to share the gospel. However, it is clear that God works through humans (in the power of the Spirit) and graciously includes us in his mission. There appears no reason to think it should be different for those with dementia, and there are ways pastors and other Christians can be better prepared for ministry to those with dementia. This will be explored more in chapter 6.

Before we go further we need to give some thought to the language and theories of cognition and knowing.

Are there helpful ways to understand how we learn and know things?[5]

Many concerns with people coming to faith in dementia come down to doubts about how people with dementia can know, remember and learn. Although this book will focus on practical and theological ways of understanding, we will encounter other schemes of knowledge. Words are used differently across these schemes, and some clarity will be required.

Philosophers often use cognition to mean any form of knowing, perception or thinking that comes from the mind

---

5   There is a huge area of intellectual endeavour devoted to the nature and philosophy of knowledge, learning, language and interpretation. My aim here is not to buy into the complexity of that endeavour, but, rather, to provide some helpful tools that make sense of how many of us experience learning, communication and 'knowing'.

or brain. It may include sensation and intuition. A number of people equate cognition with directed or controlled thought, e.g. perceiving a problem and dealing with it by rational thought. For them, while habits and intuition are ways of knowing, they are not cognitive knowledge. Knowing that the way to get from one room to another involves going through the door, rather than trying to walk through the wall, is knowing but not cognitive knowledge. I will work with this distinction between cognitive knowing and other forms of knowing.

Are there tools to help understand different ways of knowing?

I have found it helpful to work with the model of different ways of knowing advanced by Michael Polanyi.[6] Others have used similar models. Polanyi suggested there are basically two ways of knowing. 'Tacit or personal knowledge' is the knowledge we have that we either can't express or we can't express adequately. For example, I can't explain in detail why I can ride a bicycle. It's got something to do with balance, momentum and coordination. I don't know how they fit together, but I know I can ride a bicycle. So, tacit knowledge is knowledge we know we have but cannot put adequately into words.

The other form of knowledge is 'articulate knowledge'. This is knowledge that one person can effectively communicate to another. It can be encoded symbolically, in written or spoken words. This book is articulate knowledge because I am conveying ideas with words. 'Articulate knowledge' has many areas in common with cognitive knowledge.

---

6 Michael Polanyi, *Towards a Post-Critical Philosophy* (London: Routledge, 1998).

Tacit knowledge is acquired largely through experience. We know things in part by habit and experience, and respond as a result of this rather than controlling ourselves through deliberate thought.

It is important to note that these two forms of knowledge are not opposites, but are on something of a continuum.[7] We may learn something by experience and later go on to explain it adequately. When I look back I realise that I loved my wife before I put that love into words.

How does this understanding of knowledge help us?

The significance of this understanding of knowledge is that it challenges the priority given to propositional knowledge over physical, subconsciously acquired and unconsciously employed knowledge.[8] Each of you knows when you love or are loved, but you may struggle to articulate how you know this. A child knows she depends on her mother before she can put that into words. Tacit knowledge is how we know so many important things in our lives, and we need to give due weight to it when considering matters of faith, e.g. loving God and knowing we are loved by God.

It will be helpful in considering what knowledge of God is acquired or embedded through the life of someone who enters dementia without a saving faith, and how knowledge is acquired or used by God in dementia. It will also help us be open to the significance of communication that takes the

---

[7] Kenneth A. Grant shows that Polanyi is widely quoted and affirmed in subsequent publications, but is often misquoted as positing two separate forms of knowledge: 'Tacit Knowledge - We Can Still Learn from Polanyi', *The Electronic Journal of Knowledge Management* Volume 5 Issue 2, pp. 173-180, available online at www.eikm.com accessed on 1/10/2013

[8] 'Tacit Knowledge: Making it Explicit', 3, (undated) published as a working paper by The London School of Economics, at http://www.lse.ac.uk/economicHistory/Research/facts/tacit.pdf accessed on 10/08/2015.

form of facial expressions, nods, 'knowing eyes', tears and touch.

My main point here is that *articulate* knowledge of God does not represent the breadth of our knowledge of God, and an inability to articulate it is not the same as a lack of knowledge. Many carers hear and see signs of transformation and assent which fit well with the notion of *tacit* knowledge. Their stories are moving and compelling. Some are in the next chapter.

Chapter 2

The Experience of Some Carers

I spoke with a range of Christians who care for people who live with dementia. These people included nurses, chaplains, pastors and family members.[1]

The first thing that struck me was how many stories I heard of people moving from rejection of God to love and acceptance of God. I do not have statistics,[2] but rather than being a rare occurrence, conversion appears to happen often. My sister has cared for people with dementia for 35 years. In her present job, where she typically has 15 people with dementia in the mid to late stages under her care, she has seen three come to Christ in the last four years. A chaplain who serves about 150 people with dementia a year said he saw about four conversions a year. This experience challenges the view that the church and evangelism should focus on the youth as they are the most likely to come to faith.

The questions I asked
My questions were framed around the following:

---

1 This research was carried out under the guidelines for human research established by Moore College, the Universities Australia's 'Code of Conduct for Responsible Practice of Research', The Commonwealth Privacy Act (1988) and the National Health and Medical Research Council's 'Statement on Human Experimentation'.
2 It may be a valuable exercise to try to assess how many people come to faith in dementia compared with other older people, and other demographic groups. However, the statistical tools, and sources of data are beyond me.

1. Have you ever seen, heard or otherwise observed someone who did not profess Christ appear to accept Christ, or express reliance in Jesus, after being diagnosed with dementia?
2. If you pray for, or read the Bible to, someone living with dementia, have you seen any response which is different from how they usually respond (or don't respond)?
3. How, if at all, do you account for that response within your understanding of how God works to save people, including in relation to repentance, justification by faith, and knowing God?

I chose to interview carers because they are in a better position than me to assess change. We think we know what other people are thinking, based on patterns that are built up over time. People who know each other well will do this more successfully than a person will with a stranger (e.g. me). Someone who cares for another person over a time will pick up things that a stranger will not.[3] Yet, our inability to read minds and behaviour must act as a caution to this practical research.

I recognise the answers I received may also be shaped by carers misinterpreting responses, either out of hope or to justify the work they do. We should be cautious given our inability to read minds and behaviour. While some behaviour is very encouraging, we ultimately do not know whether someone comes to a saving faith. Further research could be done to control for the subjectivity that the carer brings to this conversation. This could include considering the experiences of non-Christian carers. However, as

---

3 Robert Bogdan and Steven J. Taylor, 'Relationships with Severely Disabled People: The Social Construction of Humanness', *Social Problems* 36, no. 2 (April 1989): 135-48.

mentioned above, salvation is a work of God and we cannot perfectly know anyone's relationship with God, irrespective of cognitive ability.

What changes did the carers observe?
It is typical when people enter aged care facilities, including non-religious facilities, for them to be asked if they have religious beliefs, so any beliefs can be accommodated. My sister tells the story of Marg, who was taken into care with early onset dementia. When asked if she had any religious beliefs, she said that was 'a lot of garbage, a lot of rot' and 'I want nothing to do with that!' After about a year she decided to stay for one of the church services conducted in her facility. She then went a few more times, and her son noticed a change in his mother. Marg asked him to bring in a Bible, which she began to read. By now she was regularly attending the services and my sister asked her why. Marg replied, 'I have dementia. No mortal can help me, but maybe God can', and 'God will be there. He won't walk away'. Her daughter had given up on her. As Marg's dementia progressed she could no longer read, and language had to get simpler. The Bible became her 'talking to God book'. She liked to hear 'Sunday School' stories from the Bible, about Noah, David, Daniel etc., and to look at pictures in illustrated Bibles. The decline continued. When she died she showed no sign she thought God had given up on her.

Does Bible reading help?
Peter tells the story of his father. His father had been a lifelong atheist, and developed an alcoholic-related dementia (Wernicke-Korsakoff syndrome). It was quite advanced, and he had passed beyond the stage where coherent conversation was possible. Peter realised he could

not hope to put the gospel to his father in a conventional, propositional way, and decided to read the Bible to his father, but inserted his father's name into the narrative. When he came to John 3:16, he started 'God so loved Trevor'. Before he could get the next phrase out his father said, 'I know, I know, "that he gave his only Son for me". I know that'. He would then repeat that Jesus died for him, over and over. Peter remains convinced that his father had accepted Christ and died a Christian. Peter admits that is something between his father and God, but he saw nothing in the last months to suggest that his father backed down from his statement of faith. And, of course, we can trust God to not have forgotten Trevor.

Are verbal statements of faith common?

A clear, verbal acceptance of Christ's saving work, such as the one above, was uncommon among the stories I heard, but far from unique. Bob tells the following story of his father, who had not been religious as Bob was growing up:

> "From the time my father joined the navy in WWII until he died, he never went to a church. He did not speak against religion openly, although he was quite upset when I confessed my faith back in 1974. Two years before he died, he and I had lunch. The Alzheimer's disease had already become noticeable (he could not remember directions at that point). I asked him point blank about faith and God and he said there was no God and death was the end of the story. I wrote him a letter several weeks later and his wife told me that he read it repeatedly. The following summer the Alzheimer's was much more pronounced, but

> he knew my name and other names. It was then that he told me clearly that he believed in Jesus as God's Son who died for his sin and always had. My sister ... also talked to him and he said the same to her. The following summer, he did not know much, although continued in nice conversation, often, however, with significant gaps. His complete assurance about God, Jesus, [and] salvation through faith was quite clear."

If actions speak louder than words, do people change in character when they come to trust Jesus?

Acceptance of Christ is an act of rebirth or transformation (John 3:3). Such a transformation is well evidenced in the story of Jan. Jan had been an alcoholic for many years, and had abused her children. Her children had rejected her, and never visited her because of their painful memories and because they saw no point in visiting a person 'so far gone'. When she arrived at the facility she had no faith, but gradually she started going to chapel and responding to songs of praise. In time normal speech stopped, but she would repeat, 'Blessed beautiful Jesus, Holy Son of God' and 'Beautiful Jesus'. She loved hearing about 'beautiful Jesus', and only became angry when she considered the death Jesus did not deserve. This change in attitude toward God is remarkable enough, but the thing that most sticks in the memory of her carers is the transformation in her character and behaviour that accompanied this apparent devotion to Jesus. Passivity is not uncommon in the later stages of dementia, but new-found warmth and friendliness are unusual. The staff loved being with her, and when she died she was greatly missed.

Is it ever too late?

Dementia, in the later stages, often limits the ability to communicate verbally. This is why some people think there is little hope for change in the later stages of dementia. Yet Anne, a pastoral carer, never gives up hope. She told me the story of Sue. Sue had a Catholic background, but when admitted expressed no faith. As Anne engaged with her over the next four years, they would have polite chats, but Sue would always say 'no' to any Christian engagement. Then Sue changed, and said to Anne, 'I'm the same as you'. Sue was happy to talk about Jesus and came to the chapel services Anne ran. As Sue got sicker, and was treated palliatively, she stopped talking. Anne would still sit and talk with her. As Sue neared death, Anne said, 'you know your days are numbered. Would you like me to read the Bible?' Anne knew by Sue's eye movements, movement of her mouth and other indicators that Sue was saying, 'yes'. A few days later she asked Sue if she knew about life after death. Sue said, 'yes'. This was her first coherent word for a while. Sue smiled each time Anne mentioned heaven. Anne then took her through the Gospel, that Jesus had died for her, risen from the grave and that if she believed in Jesus she would be right with God. Sue indicated by facial gesture her agreement to everything. Anne then said she would say a prayer, and said Sue could say it in her heart. When she finished, Anne asked her if that was Sue's prayer. Sue nodded and then said, 'thank you'. By this time they were both in tears. Sue took her hand from under the blankets of her bed, and reached out and touched Anne's face. Anne admits conversion is not often this clear so late in dementia, but she tenaciously believes it is never too late. She says, 'you can pray to the bitter end and they will respond'. We need to listen to the words of experience.

Anne also stressed the need to build relationships of trust. We should not dismiss babbling, but rather listen and show we care. Her view is that we bring God with us by the way we love through listening and caring, and behind babbling there is often the look of someone trying hard to communicate something that is important to them, something we may call *tacit* knowledge.

What do carers need to do?
Many carers stressed the need to get to know each person in their care. This invariably involved far more than conversation, and took a great deal of time. Of course, the question of 'how much time do we have?' has a certain potency when dealing with people who are aged, and have a terminal illness. However, many people live for a number of years with dementia, sometimes more than ten years. Most of the carers I spoke with said they often had at least 3-4 years with someone with dementia, and, therefore, they felt they had the time to develop a relationship of friendship and trust. And good things come from time spent visiting and talking, patience, kindness, reliability and prayerful persistence.

A number of providers of aged care have practical advice on how to build these relationships of friendship and trust, including HammondCare and Anglican Retirement Villages.[4]

What ways of sharing the love and good news of Jesus seem to work best?
Well constructed worship services work well with some people. Hymns and songs which people with dementia may

---

4 See HammondCare's www.hammond.com.au/LiteratureRetrieve.aspx?ID=87868 and Anglican Retirement Villages' www.arv.org.au/

have heard in their youth, or through occasional services such as weddings, baptisms and funerals, sometimes evoke more responses than Bible readings, talks and sermons. Sermons that take the form of stories, particularly if acted out, can be effective. One chaplain said he found projecting images that complement the music was very useful to some people in his care. In his view some people engaged with biblical stories through colour and imagery. He also conducts Bible studies with dementia patients, and provides them with crayons and paper. The Bible reading stimulates them to draw, and while the things drawn appear to him to have no connection with the Bible passage, he senses that they mean something to the person with dementia.

All chaplains I spoke with emphasised the power of liturgy to teach, reassure and to reactivate memories. Simple liturgies, including the Lord's Prayer, the Apostle's Creed and especially the Lord's Supper, which uses the body for expression, provide patterns of worship that are familiar and reassuring. A point to note at this stage is that words are still at the centre of ministry to people with dementia, although their use is carefully weighed, less propositional and often supplemented with music, art and enactment.

As chaplains continue to work out what works best, and specialist units develop within the Christian based aged care providers, it would be extremely helpful if they shared their experiences and insights with pastors and other Christians who care for people with dementia in their homes.

Are there any theological 'no-go areas'?
The basic principle of all evangelism, that the love and person of Jesus are the way to faith, applies equally to people with dementia. The Jesus we meet in the gospels is no less attractive in older age (or when they have early onset

dementia) than at any other time.

Some found the death of Jesus a distressing subject to discuss with some people with dementia,[5] but the sense of Christ's sacrifice on the Cross could be conveyed well through communion services, which are the most common form of service I encountered.

One retired minister who conducts services exclusively for people with dementia said he did not overtly teach groups that Jesus died for their sins, although that is the centre of his faith. His reason is that he found they did not follow, although they willingly participated in the Lord's Supper. He believed that, as they reached out their hands to take the bread and the wine, they knew they were receiving something of great importance from God. Perhaps, by hearing the words and participating in the enacted metaphor of Christ's atoning death, they acquired and/or confirmed *tacit* knowledge of the underlying truth that Christ died for them. At least they could understand that Jesus was the source of all good, they needed him and they could always rely on him.

More will be said on this below when we consider meeting people with challenging news, like that we need Jesus, when they are dealing with the stress, frustration and other emotional challenges of dementia.

None of the chaplains and carers I talked with suggested that a detailed propositional discussion of Christian doctrine or abstract ideas was a winning strategy. If we look at a range of conventional materials produced to help people understand and accept the gospel, we will find a focus on 'understanding worldviews', the historical reliability and integrity of the Bible, God as Trinity, the meaning of

---

[5] Care needs to be taken here. Some professional carers have noted that older people are not too fragile to deal with sadness and death. Protecting them from news of death may make them feel left out. Usually they have experienced far more than us.

words like 'justification', 'atonement', 'righteousness' and 'sanctification', and, sometimes, reflections on current cosmological theories. The chaplains and carers I spoke with said they rarely use these materials, not because they disagree with their theology, but for practical reasons. Rather, they talked about the love and goodness of God, the person of Jesus, and that Jesus could and wanted to help the people they cared for. They talked simply about how they could trust a God who was always reliable, always good, forgave them for the wrongs they had done, and offered them eternal life. This God was real, personal and with them. Often the character and goodness of God would be conveyed through prayers. For example, 'thank you God for making Elsa in your image. Thank you that Elsa is so special to you that you would give Jesus for her. Thank you God that you are always with us, willing to help, willing to forgive and always wanting to share your love with us, etc.' More will be said below on how this fits with our understanding of salvation by faith.

Do people with dementia approach time, and their experience of life in dementia, differently from the way others approach time and life?

One common aspect of dementia identified by carers and researchers into dementia, is that when memory and a sense of the future fail people 'live in the present' or 'live in the moment'.[6] Neither a sense of the past, nor a sense of the future, appears to shape their experience of the present.

---

[6] Swinton, *Dementia*, 235-37, 254-56. Also John Swinton, 'Being in the Moment: Developing a Contemplative approach to spiritual care with people who have dementia', pp. 175-85, in Albert Jewell ed., *Spirituality and Personhood in Dementia* (Philadelphia: Jessica Kingsley Publishers, 2011). It should be noted that 'living in the moment' is not a universal experience. Some people with dementia appear to have a heightened sense of parts of the past, which may involve living and reliving the past.

Despite the challenge this presents for carers, it also offers opportunities. For example, for an atheist or agnostic person who has advanced dementia to be told that God loves them may not come as a surprise. They may have forgotten their years of rejecting God. The memory of their life before dementia may have been lost. Their bitterness at their suffering may even be lost. Their life in the present is entirely dependent. They live in a moment that God can fill and they can know God's goodness from moment to moment.

In these situations, Gospel ministry may become more restricted, but it can still be effective. One chaplain said, for people with advanced dementia, he reduced the good news to short statements, which he repeated often in ways that would be irritating to a person who remembered how often the sound bite was repeated, but brought comfort to the patients in his care. 'God won't let you go' was one of his favourites. In the moment a patient was living in, those words worked in ways that a longer presentation could not.[7] These words seemed to be more effective than bland encouragement to 'not worry' or that 'everything will be alright'.

How can we know if someone has come to a new faith in Christ?

I know some people will object to this question – after all, what does it matter what we think! I understand that. Ultimately, for all of us, only God knows what is in our heart. At the same time, it is natural that some carers ask this question, and some carers are unnecessarily discouraged by the lack

---

7 Robert Davis writes of the value of short, repetitive sentences: *My Journey*, 110. However, another carer I discussed this with offered the caution that the people he cared for recognised patterns, and could be irritated by too much repetition.

of verbal affirmation. Also, the care we show a person will be shaped by where they are with God. For example, the need to pray for someone does not change when they accept Christ, but the content of the prayers does.

Many carers noticed the most obvious sign of a movement towards God was a new willingness to attend chapel services, to hear stories about Jesus and to receive prayer. Some verbally expressed trust in God. Others showed this by the way they talked about Jesus, in a way which showed relationship with God.

It is hard to measure church growth at the best of times, but even harder when many in the congregation die each year. However, one chaplain mentioned he had seen significant growth from 30 to 50 in his dementia centre. About 98% of the residents in his care had a cognitive impairment, and the average length of stay was about 19 months. So growth can be substantial!

The chaplains I spoke with emphasised the need to engage with people in many different ways, and recognise different signs of acceptance of God. My sister stressed the need to 'enter into the world' of the people in her care. She cared for one person who had advanced dementia, and lived through two toy dolls. To get her up in the morning, she would respond to 'baby needs to get up'. To get her to eat, she would respond to 'it's time for baby to eat'. One doll she called 'baby Jesus'. She would rock him, and cuddle him, and coo to her 'baby Jesus'. Was this the way she showed her love of God? Perhaps only God knows.

These are only a few of the many wonderful stories I heard. Perhaps, for some, this book would be more encouraging if I told many more of these stories, or perhaps only told those stories. As a pastor, I love telling stories about how God works in people's lives. But I am also conscious that many of the people I spoke with have questions about the intersection of their experience of people with dementia, and the theology of salvation, and would like some help with these questions. So, it is now time to think about how dementia affects us, and what that might mean for our relationships with the God who saves.

Chapter 3

The Effects of Dementia

In this chapter I will consider some further questions about whether dementia rules out someone coming to a saving faith. I will look at what dementia does to, and what it means for, someone who acquires it. But I will first consider the things people with dementia have in common with all other people.

Is there anything inherent in dementia that precludes the saving work of Jesus?
Some Christians will consider this a nonsense question. After all, God is all powerful and all good, and nothing in his creation could possibly limit him. True, but I think it is useful to consider it, because it helps us get into thinking about how we are all dependent on the goodness and power of God. For someone with dementia is no more dependent on the grace of God for salvation than any other person. This is because both are totally dependent on that grace.

All people are dependent in the sense that their lives are contingent on God sustaining them from moment to moment: 'For in God we live and move and have our being' (Acts 17:28). And they are dependent in the sense that knowledge of God and faith are gifts of God for the well and those with dementia.

Faith is not earned because of our capacities, goodness or works (Romans 3:10; 4:13-25). Jesus says we are to come to him as children (Matthew 18:3; Luke 18:17; also Matthew 11:25), which speaks both of childlike dependence and undeveloped cognitive ability. In John's gospel we hear him tell his disciples that apart from him they can do nothing (John 15:5). Coming to Jesus is always expressed to be a work of the Holy Spirit (John 6:63; Acts 10:44; Romans 8:26; Galatians 4:6 and many others) in ways that preclude the privileging of self-will and cognition that is evident in other systems of salvation.

How does God reach someone with dementia, and will he show us how he does it?

We read that Jesus came to seek and save the lost (Luke 19:10), but how does this work for a person with dementia?

Perhaps we can look at the way Jesus reaches the demon possessed man in the region of the Gerasenes (Luke 8:26-39), to see the power, adaptability and appropriateness of Jesus' response to the needs of the lost. There are obvious differences, as we do not today associate dementia with demon possession, and the man called Jesus the 'son of the Most High God'. Yet there are some points of comparison. The demon-possessed man was, in the minds of some, sub-human. He was uncontrollable, relationally barren and cognitively deficient. When he was naked and he broke the shackles it appears he did not recognise pain. To some his sub-human condition may have suggested he was beyond salvation—but not for Jesus. Jesus did not engage the man with a verbal presentation of the gospel, or, on the evidence, call on him to repent and believe. Rather he dealt with the needs of the man and the problem he was facing. He restored him physically, mentally and relationally. The man ended up in his right mind, and at the feet of Jesus. Perhaps we should see this only as an example of the grace and power of God, although I am inclined to see it as a bit more than that. Jesus brought salvation to a mentally disabled and relationally desperate person, although not by conventional means. We saw similar signs of grace-filled restoration in some of the stories in chapter 2.

> Some people I have discussed this story with in the context of dementia have noted that for many centuries it would have been common to discuss mental illness and demon possession together. Others are offended by it. My purpose is not to cause offence, but only to show, without in any way equating dementia and demon possession, that God can save in the most desperate situations. However, the response of offence shows that the link between mental illness and demons is rarely discussed and often poorly understood. In the story in Luke 13:10-17, Jesus appears to equate all disability and illness with the work of Satan. I cannot think of a good reason to exclude mental illness from this. It seems to me that, as Satan will use anything to lead us away from Jesus, we should not be surprised if he tries to use mental illness to do that. Of course, as God can thwart the best plans of Satan, we should expect him to not allow mental illness to lead us away from Jesus or stop us coming to him.

With this introduction, I think the question of God's grace towards people with dementia can take a different shape depending on how it is framed. We may say, 'we preach the gospel of grace'. Because of the increased dependence of a person with dementia, we may hope God would do something in his/her life that he does not do in the life of a person who wilfully continues in rebellion. However, another view may be, 'why should we expect God to do something in the life of someone who rebelled all their healthy life just because they now live with dementia?' Neither approach is very satisfactory. As people with and without dementia are both totally dependent on God at all times, *dependence* and God's saving grace are good places to start.

If we are dependent, don't we need to know we are?
We should not insist on cognition of our dependence. Knowing our dependence on God may be a wonderful aspect of faith for someone for whom 'cognitive knowing' is easy, but 'knowing dependence' is still different from the experience of dependence. Dependence may be *tacit* knowledge, acquired by experience, including the experience of dementia. God sees both *articulate* and *tacit* dependence, and can be expected to deal with each person according to our needs and abilities. This will be explored further in chapter 5.

What is dementia?
There are two common, and largely similar, definitions of dementia. The World Health Organisation's International Classification of Diseases (ICD-10) defines it as:

> *"A syndrome due to disease of the brain, usually of a chronic or progressive nature, in which there is a disturbance of multiple higher cortical functions, including memory, thinking, orientating, comprehension, calculation, learning capability, language and judgement. Consciousness is not impaired. Impairments of cognitive function are commonly accompanied, and occasionally preceded, by deterioration in emotional control, social behaviour, or motivation."* [1]

---

1 The ICD-10 Classification of Mental and Behavioural Disorders: Clinical Descriptions

There are said to be about 100 forms of dementia, of which Alzheimer's disease is probably the most common and best known.[2] In this book I will refer to 'dementia' generically, although I recognise that the different diseases, and, indeed, different people, will require more nuanced responses and ways of understanding behaviour.

What do we know about dementia?

A lot of research has been and is being undertaken on dementia. As is often the case, the more we learn the more we realise what we don't know.

That said, there is currently no cure for dementia, and the disease is always terminal.[3] As mentioned above, 'dementia' is an umbrella term for a large number of individual diseases. Some people get 'early-onset' dementia in their thirties, forties and fifties, but it is most common in people over 70.[4] The disease is progressive. Although there is no standard pattern, as the different disease profiles are distinct, people often start with impairment of the short term memory, progress through a stage of anxiety and growing emotional detachment as they are less able to access their memories, and end in 'advanced' dementia. This may involve an absence of coherent conversation and control over bodily functions, including eating and breathing. The

---

and Diagnostic Guidelines (Geneva: World Health Organisation, 1992). The alternative medical definition is published by the American Psychiatric Association: Diagnostic and Statistical Manual of Mental Disorders, 4th Edition, Text Revision, also known as *DSM-IV-TR*

2 See website of Alzheimer's Australia: http://www.fightdementia.org.au/understanding-dementia/types-of-dementia.aspx

3 Post, *Moral*, 2. People with dementia often die of other causes, such as cancer or pneumonia, but there is, as yet, no cure.

4 In Australia 1.2% of the population is affected by dementia. This may increase to 2.8% by 2050: Productivity Commission, *Caring For Older Australians*, 42. Up to 50% of people over 85 can expect to experience some form of dementia: Post, *Moral*, 2.

characteristic of both definitions of dementia is 'loss' or 'defect'. The losses of intellectual, linguistic and cognitive function are linked to molecular and cellular decline in the brain.[5]

What are some practical limitations of scientific knowledge?
'Dementia' means 'loss of mind', which itself is misleading and unhelpful. First, it labels our perception of the problems a person is facing, and neurological changes, as 'loss of mind', with no evidence that the 'mind' (whatever that is) is lost to the person or to God. Second, it too quickly gets us thinking that 'loss of mind' must mean loss of 'self' and loss of 'personhood'. Dementia is seen by many as a form of death. We need to be careful to ensure this view does not shape the way we value and think about people with dementia.

The medical definition takes an approach based on deficit. There is nothing wrong with medical science taking this approach. It is directed towards the recognition of the disease, the amelioration of symptoms and the ultimate cure of the disease. However, neurologists present only one perspective on dementia. Neurology cannot account for carers' observations of changed confessions and character. Nor does it allow for the loving relationships that develop between carers and the people in their care.

We should recognise the limitations of science. Despite the remarkable contribution of modern medical science, we simply do not know what another person is thinking. Even brain scans which show a lack of activity in areas that are usually associated with some types of neurological

---

[5] Richard Cheston and Michael Bender, *Understanding Dementia: The Man with the Worried Eyes*, (London: Jessica Kingsley Publishers, 1999), 67.

thought do not 'prove' a lack of thought, and clearly have no capacity to measure how a person is 'thinking' about or how they relate with God or another person. Christians do not doubt that a dead person is in some sense with God, 'asleep', 'resting with Jesus' or at least in some way preserved for ultimate resurrection.[6] Theologically there is no reason why scientific recognition of some neurological damage should mean 'loss of mind' when death does not. This is not to suggest we should accept some form of thinking that sees 'body' and 'mind' as two separate spheres of existence.[7] Rather we need to look at the way that we always exist in some way in God and yet, for as long as we draw breath, a person is present.

What do we learn or come to remember in dementia?

It is hard to assess what memories people acquire in dementia, or how *tacit* knowledge operates or changes in dementia, but we should never assume someone does not know or remember what is said and done. While it may appear some do not remember something from moment to moment, there can be both engagement in the moment and startling moments of lucidity and memory.[8] This particularly seems to be the case with music, emotions and pictures, but it can be quite varied.[9] People with dementia can love in the

---

6 See, for example, some of the options in Nicholas Thomas Wright, *Surprised by Hope: Rethinking Heaven, the Resurrection, and the Mission of the Church* (New York: Harper Collins, 2008), 13-30.

7 This approach based on two spheres of existence is often called 'Platonic' dualism. For a detailed discussion of life after death, the intermediate state, the different forms of dualism and why 'holistic dualism' is biblically sound, see John W. Cooper, *Body, Soul, and Life Everlasting: Biblical Anthropology and the Monism-Dualism Debate* (Grand Rapids: Eerdmans, 1989).

8 This is mentioned in a number of studies, e.g. Davis, *Journey*, 81, Swinton, *Dementia*, 237, and was confirmed in the interviews I undertook.

9 See Noel Clifford Schultz, *Forgetting but not Forgotten* (Adelaide: Openbook, 2004), 30-31

moment and enjoy God from moment to moment. There is also growing evidence for the ability to learn or relearn skills with appropriate teaching.

How 'lost' are memories?
A more comprehensive answer is given at pp.56-58, However, although the medical definitions of dementia include 'loss of memory', care needs to be taken with this as it is too all-embracing. Often the first thing that goes is short-term memory, and this can be deeply frustrating and challenging. However, long-term memory can survive into the very late stages of dementia. A person may not be able to articulate memories, but many of the stories I heard were about people responding to pictures, music or songs either from their youth or which triggered associations with their youth. I vividly recall one chapel service in which a woman with dementia sat in a wheel chair. She was curled in on herself, and said nothing but a few quietly babbled sounds. Yet when the first notes of the hymn *All Hail the Power of Jesus' Name* were played she uncurled, looked up, smiled, and then sang every word of every verse from memory. Sceptics may account for this by saying the mind can randomly misfire, but it appears to happen too often with Christian songs and liturgy to be coincidence.

Conclusion
When we start with our eternal dependence of God, and his power and desire to reach us in all our conditions, rather than a definition based on deficit, we start to see things more from God's perspective than our own experience of life in this age, with its share of delights, but also its share

of brokenness and disappointment. We will pursue God's perspective on us more in the next chapter, particularly his view of what it means to be a human person, and where our memories fit in with his view of our personhood.

Chapter 4

Personhood, Self, Memory and Resurrection

Dementia poses questions to personhood, identity and faith:

- If being 'me' is related in some important ways to my memory, who will I be if I can no longer access my memory?
- If I cannot access my memory, will it still exist?
- Is my memory only matter functioning in a particular way?
- If my mind is essential to who I am, what am I if I lose my mind?
- If I am not me, am I still a person?
- How can I have faith, or a personal relationship with God, if I can't think, communicate or recognise the people I once loved?
- How can I repent when I can't remember what I have done and don't know the difference between right and wrong?

To address these questions we need both to counter unchristian views of *personhood* and to present a Christian view of *personhood*. For, if there is no *person*, there is no one to save. This consideration of *personhood* will need to address the concepts of *mind, memory, self-perception* and *body/soul* dualism. I will then consider how we can understand 'knowing God' in dementia.

What are some unchristian perspectives on personhood? What are we fighting against?

The atheist philosopher Peter Singer argues that *personhood* should not be recognised in someone who lacks the capacity for 'self-awareness, self-control, a sense of the future, a sense of the past, the capacity to relate to others, concern for others, communication, and curiosity'.[1] Thus, those who lose these capacities should be euthanised as they are an unnecessary cost to society.[2] Singer is not alone. Baroness Warnock has advocated killing people 'because the real person has already gone and all that's left is the body of the person'.[3]

English philosopher John Harris argues that a person is 'a creature capable of valuing its own existence', and, if he/she is unable to do so in a sustained manner, he/she ceases to be a person.[4]

Each of these views embodies hyper-cognition ('an excessive emphasis on intellect and cognition') and hyper-memory ('an excessive emphasis on memory'),[5] such that to have dementia is to lose one's *personhood*. It involves the prioritising of cognition over moral or social significance, or God's view of humanity.

A further challenge for these views is that they fail to clarify when a person with a diagnosis of dementia fails to be a human. For example what level of cognition is required to be considered a human, and who should be given the

---

[1] Singer, *Practical Ethics*, 83.
[2] For a discussion of this see Keith G. Meador and Shaun C. Henson, in Hauerwas, *Growing*, 90-128.
[3] Jackie Macadam, 'Interview with Mary Warnock: "A Duty to Die"', *Life and Work*, 2008, 23-25 at 25.
[4] John Harris, 'The Concept of Person and the Value of Life', *Kennedy Institute of Ethics Journal 9*, no. 4 (1999), 293-308 at 307.
[5] Post, *Moral*, 3 and Swinton, *Dementia*, 110.

unhappy task of deciding? Do we leave the decision to emotionally exhausted relatives, or doctors who need another bed?

How pervasive are these views?

Singer and Harris may be on an extreme end of a spectrum of views, but aspects of their understanding of personhood are quite common. Some carers speak of, 'the lights being on but no one is there'. Some people with dementia fear they are no longer themselves when they cannot remember things.[6] Chaplains report that they regularly deal with families who justify not visiting their loved one because they are 'not really there', or because they are no longer named by their loved one. Yet the same people delight in visiting infant members of their families who also do not recognise them.

If not 'capacity', how should we determine personhood?

The views of Singer, Warnock, Harris and others are based on the view that *personhood* is determined by cognition. They say a lack of cognitive capacity equates to a lack of *personhood*. Tom Kitwood takes a different approach. He describes *personhood* as a 'standing or status that is bestowed upon one human being by others in the context of relationship and social being. It implies recognition, respect and trust'.[7] It grows out of a recognition that the greatest loss a person can suffer with dementia is relationship and respect rather than losing cognition. Compared with definitions based on capacity, this is a significant improvement. However, it is no help for the person who no one knows or cares about. It

---

6   Davis, *Journey*, 121-28. Also MacKinlay, *Spiritual Dimension*, 150.
7   Thomas Kitwood, *Dementia Reconsidered: The Person Comes First* (Buckingham: Open University Press, 1997), 8, quoted in Swinton, *Dementia*, 140.

seems that Kitwood's definition still permits the category of non-person.[8]

Taking human-centred approaches to *personhood* creates a range of problems. Whether we focus on capacities or relationships, we place humans as both law maker and judge, and, in the case of euthanasia, executioner.

What is the 'mind'?
Swinton makes what he calls a 'deeply practical observation' that we don't know whether anyone has a *mind*.[9] We see behaviour which we attribute to a *mind*, and when that behaviour becomes unrecognisable we say, 'they have lost their mind', when all we mean is that we cannot recognise it any longer. Swinton argues that we don't know from the outputs, or lack of outputs, from a person with dementia that thinking is impaired. Articulation and expression may be impaired, but it does not follow that *tacit* knowledge is impaired.

We can be too quick to think that conversation has ended, when the regular 'to-and-fro' of everyday speech is missing. To have a conversation with someone with dementia takes at least the following steps:

1. Hear the sounds and/or watch the body language.
2. Translate the sounds/body language into a meaningful message.
3. Understand the message.
4. Create a meaningful concept as a response.
5. Translate the meaningful concept into words/body language.
6. Articulate these words/body language in the right

---

8 See criticisms in Swinton, *Dementia*, 144.
9 Swinton, *Dementia*, 59.

language (taking into consideration the cultural and linguistic context).
7. Hear the sounds and/or watch the body language of the person/people you are communicating with.

All this takes time and patience. A failure at any one step will result in an impaired conversation. But, even then, an impaired conversation does not mean impaired thinking, because we simply never know what another person is thinking.

Isn't the 'mind' like a computer?
We are used to the ideas of hardware and software. *Memory* is sometimes equated with the files of a computer, which a fully-functioning mind both sustains and accesses.[10] A diseased mind experiences both the corruption of those files and an inability to consistently access the files that are left.[11] Hence, *memory* is seen entirely as a product of our brains (i.e. neurological matter). The same is true of *self*. The lack of the ability to articulate access to *memory* is equated with the loss of self-perception, and, with that, the loss of *self* and *personhood*.

What is a Christian perspective on personhood and knowing?
The key to dealing with these complex issues from a Christian perspective is to understand *personhood* from

---

10 For example, see Paul Ricouer, *Memory, History, Forgetting*, trans. Kathleen Blamey and David Pellauer (Chicago: Chicago University Press, 2004), 4, and Miroslav Volf, *The End of Memory: Remembering Rightly in a Violent World* (Grand Rapids: Eerdmans, 2006), 67-68. Both these writers have some very interesting things to say about memory. They are part of a much bigger discussion about how memories work that is beyond the scope of this paper. For a biblical theology of memory, see Keck, *Forgetting*, 43-70. Also of value is Brevard Childs, *Memory and Tradition in Israel* (London: SCM Press, 1962).
11 Keck speaks of the disease 'eroding' memories, and the 'tape being wiped', *Forgetting*, 21 and 58.

God's perspective, as God forms and sustains all life and is the agent of conversion and resurrection. For, if God sees a *person*, he may save that person.

Who is a 'person' in God's eyes?

In the Bible we see that a *person* is someone God makes in his image for relationship with himself (Genesis 1:27; 2:15-17; 3:8-10; 1 Corinthians 11:7; James 3:9-10). Whether we value our selves (or others), we (and they) are still a *person* to God, and therefore valuable, and capable of being both loved and saved (Romans 8:26-30). To God it seems that the essence of human life is not *mind* but being animated by the Spirit's breath of life and bearing his image. It appears, from God's perspective, that human life is dust plus breath (Genesis 2:7).

Don't we have bodies and souls? What if we lose our soul?

The concept of human life often gets caught up in talk of 'souls', and the idea that the *soul* is the immortal dimension of the human person. This is not only unhelpful, it is very different from the biblical view of 'soul'. As Wendell Berry observed, 'The dust, formed as man and made to live, did not embody a soul; it became a soul'.[12] This is because the general sense of *soul* in both Testaments is 'life' or 'possessing life'.

On the few occasions when 'soul' is used with another aspect of being it never suggests a division within a whole person. In Jeremiah 32:41, 'all my heart and soul' means 'all of me', as do similar phrases in Mark 12:30 and Luke 10:27. In Mark 12:29, Jesus magnificently answers the question asked

---

[12] Wendell Berry, *The Art of the Commonplace: The Agrarian Essays of Wendell Berry* (Berkeley: Counterpoint Press, 2002), 313, quoted in Swinton, *Dementia*, 167.

by a teacher of the Law, 'Of all the commandments, which is the most important?' by quoting from Deuteronomy 6:4-5:

> *"The most important one," answered Jesus, "is this: 'Hear, O Israel: The Lord our God, the Lord is one. Love the Lord your God with all your heart and with all your soul and with all your mind and with all your strength."*

Jesus was not suggesting that it was possible to love God with your soul and not your heart or your mind. He was emphasising the need to love God with our whole being.

Equally, more expanded phrases like 'all your heart and with all your soul and with all your strength and with all your mind' (Luke 10:26) are simply ways of emphatically talking about the whole being, and aspects of that whole being. In 1 Corinthians 6 Paul is at pains to show that our bodies are essential parts of our total beings, so much so that he can call our bodies temples of the Holy Spirit. What we do with our bodies sexually is just as important to God as the devotion we seek in our minds. We cannot separate our bodies from our minds, and live a dual existence. Similarly, we read in James 2:14-17:

> *"What good is it, my brothers and sisters, if someone claims to have faith but has no deeds? Can such faith save them? Suppose a brother or a sister is without clothes and daily food. If one of you says to them, "Go in peace; keep warm and well fed," but does nothing about their physical needs, what good is it? In the same way, faith by itself, if it is not accompanied by action, is dead."*

The deeds James contemplates are things we do with our bodies for the good of other people. Faith is intrinsic to, and an expression of, our whole being.

These passages do not suggest *body*, *soul* and *spirit* are separate realties of existence while there is a body. Our *souls* are not separate from our bodies, except in death. And, our *souls* die in death. That is, the totality of our being experiences death (remembering that Jesus shows us that death is not total annihilation, but a significant transition to another form of existence). We are, in a sense, 'with God/disembodied' before conception, then embodied *souls* until death, then disembodied *souls* in the intermediate state, then re-embodied *souls* in the resurrection.[13] However, we are never a combination of parts, or less than a whole. In life, 'We are our bodies as we are our souls'.[14] Therefore, it appears that God's perspective is that, while there is breath, a human cannot lose their *personhood* in dementia.[15] While there is breath there is human life, *personhood* and hope. That is the perspective of the God who creates, sustains and saves, and it is both more hopeful and far more important than human perspectives on *personhood*.

---

13 I am aware that caution is required in discussing existence, death and resurrection in these ways. We need to be careful to not develop dogmatic statements out of Bible passages that are directed at different purposes. For example, references to God's foreknowledge of us suggest we had an existence in God before we were conceived. However, while these references seem to serve the primary purpose of assurance or encouragement, they do suggest there is some basis for thinking of a 'pre-conception' existence (Romans 8:29; 11:2 and 1 Peter 1:2). Similar care needs to be taken with references to the end of life and resurrection. We read that Jesus is the 'first-fruits' of the resurrection, and we will receive new bodies (1 Corinthians 15:20), but we do not know with certainty the nature of our existence 'in paradise' (Luke 23:43) prior to the general resurrection.
14 Swinton, *Dementia*, 167.
15 There is not space here to deal with the challenges that arise from the artificial extension of 'life' by respirators etc.

Aren't we what we think?

Many of us have been so shaped by the Enlightenment, that we sub-consciously affirm views such as Descartes, 'I think, therefore I am'. We doubt what we will be if we cannot think the way we usually think.

In Galatians 4:8-9 Paul draws a distinction between a pre-Christian existence, that is, 'when you did not know God', and a Christian existence, 'now that you know God – or rather are known by God'. From this distinction, it appears 'we' are what God knows, not what we think about ourselves. It may be hard to let go of our self-identity, but it seems that God's view of us is more valuable than our own sense of self.

With this in mind, we can see that our existence and status before God is not determined by how much we know about him (i.e. factual knowledge), but our relationship with him. James K. A. Smith puts it this way:

> *"Being a disciple of Jesus is not primarily a matter of getting the right ideas and doctrines into our head in order to guarantee proper behaviour; rather it's a matter of being the kind of person who loves rightly – who loves God and neighbour and is orientated to the world by the primacy of that love."* [16]

This type of response to God fits well with the idea of *tacit* knowledge, and offers hope to someone who has problems with their memory, or expressing what they know.

Our *personhood* is not determined by the discretion of other humans, but by God. A human does not lose their *personhood* when he/she has forgotten who they are.[17]

---

16 *Desiring*, 32-33. The relationship of this behaviour to *faith* is discussed in chapter 5.
17 See Swinton, *Dementia*, 89-91.

When my brain doesn't work as it used to, won't I lose my 'inner-self'?

It seems that many of us have a sense of an 'inner-me' and the 'me' we show to the outside world. This can lead us to identify *personhood* with an *inner-self*, or the sense of self-perception.

However, *inner* and *outer* are aspects of personhood or 'natures', but not separate identities.[18] We need to get away from the idea that the real 'me' is an *inner-self*, separate from my body and the way the whole of me relates to others. We are relational beings, so 'who I am' is tied in with others, including God. I am who I am in relation to God, whether I am at a particular moment of time a Christian or not. God did not suddenly get interested in me at the age of 30 when I became a Christian. I have always been in his thoughts (Romans 8:29-30, 12:2; Ephesians 1:5, 11). Therefore, I have always had an existence, but that existence is tied up with God, rather than being tied to my body, my brain, my self-perception or my ability to articulate that self-perception.

A focus on the electro-chemical workings of the brain does not help us much in understanding God's perspective on our personhood. Swinton puts it well when he says that *personhood* is an 'irrevocable status that comes from being a human being', and nothing can make him/her less than a person.[19] Based on Romans 8:38-39, we could add, 'including death'. If death does not destroy *personhood*, then dementia certainly cannot. It seems that there is no suggestion that persons ever change their God-given status

---

18 Michael Hill, *The Heart of Marriage: Loving Your Wife with a Christian Mind* (Sydney South, NSW: Aquila Press, 2013), 27.

19 The term 'human being' is far less controversial. It simply means a man, woman, or child of the species Homo sapiens. In other words, it is someone who is born to human parents.

as persons. They never cease to bear the image of God. Even the ghastly pictures of judgement and separation from God we see in Matthew 25:12, 30 and 46 do not imply a loss of status as humans or *personhood*.

Is science useless then?
No, not at all. We need science to help manage and cure dementia, but science is not capable of testing or bestowing *personhood*.

We cannot draw theological conclusions from medical observation, diagnosis and self-assessment. As mentioned above, because scans may show damage to the parts of the brain that we think deal with memory and communication, and people have difficulty showing that they have access to their memories, it is thought that people are 'losing their memories'. However, at worst, they are only losing access to their memories for a while. Ben Bolan works with people with dementia and says, 'I think of [loss of brain function] in terms of an amputee who has truly lost a leg but who is not defined by the loss and who can look toward to walking, leaping and dancing in heaven'.

Isn't losing our memories so like death that we might as well treat it as death?
I am sorry to persist with such negative questions, but, as they are asked, they need to be answered. And the answer is a clear 'no'. We have no reason to believe God equates our loss of access to our memories as death or 'loss of *personhood*'.

However, the theology of death can help us understand the relationship between memory and dementia. The theology of death is that it is not the end of us. When the creeds proclaim a belief in the resurrection of the body, and we speak of re-creation (Revelation 21; esp. 21:5), we do not think we will be totally new persons.

It was Jesus who rose from the grave – not a new, different person who looked like him (John 20:11-21:24). He had the same capacities to think and communicate and remember when he met his disciples on the first Easter as he took to the cross. We read in 1 Corinthians 15:20-23:

> *"But Christ has indeed been raised from the dead, the first-fruits of those who have fallen asleep. For since death came through a man, the resurrection of the dead comes also through a man. For as in Adam all die, so in Christ all will be made alive. But each in turn: Christ, the first-fruits; then, when he comes, those who belong to him."*

The first-fruit is the promise of the abundance that will follow. Jesus was raised in a new, magnificent, body, equipped for eternity, but bearing the scars of his death, and recognisable to his friends. In the same way, we expect to be 'us' when we rise after death, not people who look like we looked but are totally different people. When Jesus turned to the criminal who was crucified with him, and said, 'today you will be with me in paradise', we take it that he meant that both he and the criminal would be themselves, not some other persons, in paradise, despite the awful death they were both about to endure (Luke 23:43).

What happens to our memories at death?

Our brains stop working. In time they cease to exist. In order that we can be resurrected as 'us', something must happen to our memories. It makes most sense to believe that God protects our memories through death so that we are resurrected as 'us'. While recognising that all human memories are frail, God's knowledge of us is complete (Psalm 139:1). The Psalmist says of God, 'You know my thoughts even when I'm far away' (Psalm 139:2). Thus, our memories are with God.[20] We are not ultimately dependent on the functioning of our brains, or our own wills, capacities or human relationships. We are dependent on the God of salvation and resurrection

Being resurrected with access to our memories is necessary so we can give an account of our lives on judgement day (2 Corinthians 6:10), but it is also essential to the eternal lives *we* will lead. In God's grace and time, we are re-embodied. We can assume that whatever access we need to our memories will be re-embodied with us. To the extent our memories include our thoughts, responses, habits and other aspects of our being, God is always able to resurrect the 'me' that is somehow constituted by those thoughts, responses, habits etc.

Yet it is hard to believe we will be resurrected with every thought we have ever had. In normal life we do not remember everything, and we reshape parts of our memories. My faith has replaced my rebellion. My happiness is shaped by God's gift of forgiveness that allows me to forget, or put aside, my acts and thoughts of brokenness. Similarly we could expect that a recognition and acceptance of dependence, and a new love of God, acquired in dementia, will form part of the life to come. It will 'override' the rebellion and rejection that preceded it, because that is how God perceives the person carrying his image, and that is how we may think of God re-embodying us.

---

20 Swinton writes extensively on this subject, and it is one of his major contributions to understanding God's relationship with people with dementia: *Dementia*, 186-226. See also Keck, *Forgetting*, 124.

Aren't our memories important then?

Yes, they are important. But just because dementia may harm our ability to access them in the last years of life, it does not mean they are lost. Both theologically and experientially, our memories ultimately are with God and are not contingent on our brains. Further, God's ability and willingness to save is not limited by any general reliance on *articulate* ways of knowing and not hindered by our temporary loss of access to our memories.

Compared to being held in the memory of God, our immediate access to our memories and the ability to articulate our knowledge seems quite fragile.

Don't we need our brains to experience God?

We sense the brain is significant in our experience of the spiritual dimension of life. This is particularly the case for those who come from and have benefitted through Christian traditions which emphasise thought and logic. Again, turning to the Bible helps us work this through. Rather than the brain being the source of spiritual enquiry and satisfaction, God is. It is God who gives us a sense that life is more than matter. He reveals the divine (Romans 1:18-20). It is God's Spirit who moves us towards him (Romans 8:27), and it is, '*the Spirit who sustains us in our spirituality and in our identity*' (emphasis original).[21]

Diminished brain function may impact the experience of this. Various people have written on the challenges and frustrations this brings to Christians who enter dementia.[22] However, the experience of some people with dementia and their carers is that the enjoyment of the spiritual can

---

21 Swinton, *Dementia*, 174.
22 Davis, *Journey*, and McKinlay, *Spiritual*.

be enhanced and sustained in dementia.[23] Either way, as the Spirit sustains us, dementia cannot remove the spiritual dimension of life, and we can see that human identity is 'both given and sustained by the Holy Spirit'.[24]

How does dementia affect our reception of God's grace?

People with dementia are the same people at the various stages of dementia as they are when they enter it, and as they will be in the resurrection. Throughout that they can be subject to the work of the Holy Spirit, as we shall see in chapter 5.

What does the Bible say about knowing God in dementia?

Medical science and the way we think about the brain have changed greatly since biblical times. It is difficult to equate the description of anyone we meet in the Bible with what we would call 'dementia'.

Yet Romans 8:38-39 is pregnant with hope for people who enter dementia as believers, and equally offers hope for someone who comes to Christ in dementia:

> *"For I am convinced that neither death nor life, neither angels nor demons, neither the present nor the future, nor any powers, neither height nor depth, nor anything else in all creation, will be able to separate us from the love of God that is in Christ Jesus our Lord."*

---

23 Christine Bryden and Elizabeth MacKinlay, 'Dementia: A Spiritual Journey Towards the Divine: A Personal View of Dementia', *Journal of Religious Gerontology 13*, issue 3 and 4 (2003), 69-75, 72.

24 Here Swinton is summarising the work of Ray Anderson in *Whatever Happened to the Soul? Scientific and Theoretical Portraits of Human Nature*, ed. Warren S. Brown, Nancy Murphy, and H. Newton Malony (Minneapolis: Fortress Press, 1998): Swinton, *Dementia*, 175.

In the original context, Paul was referring to elect Jews, including those who had not come to trust Jesus. To extrapolate from this, we could say that nothing will separate the elect who live with dementia from the love of God, even if they are currently not yet Christian. And 'nothing' includes dementia!

Perhaps Psalm 88:12 raises doubt:

> *"Are your wonders known in the place of darkness,*
> *or your righteous deeds in the land of oblivion?"*

Yet, 'the place of darkness' and the 'land of oblivion' are metaphors for death, not mental illness. There is nothing here to suggest that God's glorious light cannot shine into the life of someone with dementia.

How might God see our knowing?

Two cautions are necessary. First, we don't know how God sees our knowing. Second, it is clear, both from my studies and the studies of others,[25] that understanding other people 'is always subjective and never totally accessible to others'.[26]

When considering how God may interact with a person with dementia we should remember that conversion in the Bible is not primarily the acquisition of *articulate* knowledge. It is not a change from 'I don't think Jesus is Lord and saviour' to 'I do think Jesus is Lord and saviour', although it can be expressed in these terms (e.g. John 20:28).

It is a change in relationship, being 'born again' in the words of Jesus to Nicodemus (John 3:1-15). It is a change

---

[25] For example, Robert Bogdan and Steven J. Taylor, 'Relationships with severely disabled People: The Social Construction of Humanness', Social Problems 36, no.2 (April 1989): 135-48.
[26] Bogdan and Taylor, 'Relationships', 139.

of status from enemy to adopted child (Romans 5:10, 8:10; Galatians 4:5; Ephesians 1:5).

The next step is to realise the relationship is initiated by God. Karl Barth expressed it well when he said that God has found a way to us.[27] For each person, their knowledge of God is shaped and filled out by God.

Why might we think that God will save people with dementia?
We have no reason to believe that dementia changes God's capacity and willingness to save. If anything, one could argue that, as our dependence on him increases, and, as the malignancy of our earthly thinking gets stripped away, it may even be more likely that God may act. If there is little or no access to memory, there is no distraction of 'self', and the denial of God's claim that is the heart of sin.

When we 'live in the moment' we may have thoughts neither of the past nor the future. While anxiety and selfishness can be manifestations of some forms of dementia in some stages, when 'living in the moment' we may be in a more responsive state in which to experience dependence on God. The concerns of this world will not get in the way. Through this experience, we may *tacitly* know dependence.

Knowing the overwhelming goodness of God, we can believe that people with dementia are still loved by God. Christ died for them regardless of their physical or psychological condition. We see this in Paul's words of assurance to all believers: 'though our outer self is wasting away, our inner self is being renewed day by day' (2 Corinthians 4:16). We should not make this assurance conditional on a person in dementia being able to articulate their sense of that renewal. Some people with a dementia diagnosis will be able to

---

27 *Dogmatics in Outline* (London: SCM, 2001).

articulate their faith just as some people without dementia will struggle or even be unable to articulate their faith.

How can a person with dementia know God if he/she does not recognise people he/she once knew and loved, e.g. a spouse or child?

It is sad to hear stories of people with dementia not recognising their spouses or children. Recognition is obviously very important to the way we usually relate to each other. Two things may be said. First, recognition may be tied up in *tacit* knowledge, to which observers have limited access. Second, the evidence in chapter 2 suggests that God can make himself known 'to the bitter end'. Failing neurology may make it difficult for carers to maintain relationships with people with dementia, but as with the story of Jesus and the demon-possessed man, these relational challenges are not beyond God.

Pastorally it is also important that our love for people should not be conditional on the response we get back from them. A person with cognitive decline may not recognise a loved one, or may recognise them but be unable to find the name of the person. (Many of us struggle to remember the names of some people at times, but it does not mean we do not appreciate them!).

Conclusion

This Christian view of personhood should free carers of anxiety. When carers love people who are affected by dementia, they may be loving people who are known to God and who know God. With that in mind, it is now time to look at how understanding 'justification by grace alone through faith' in dementia can further free carers from anxiety, so they know their work will have eternal significance.

Chapter 5

Salvation by Grace

In this chapter I will look at *faith*, and consider its relation to cognition and knowledge. I will also consider other possible theological objections to coming to Christ in dementia.

What do we need to do/be/think/believe to be saved?
It is hard to answer this question without thinking of Matthew 19:16-27, when Jesus is asked, 'Teacher, what good thing must I do to get eternal life?'. I don't have that in mind with this question, although we should note Jesus' words of comfort that, 'with God all things are possible'. When I ask this question I am thinking more about what 'faith', in the sense of 'justification by faith alone', looks like.

We are saved when we come to faith. That salvation will be consummated on Judgement Day in the welcome God will extend to all who believe (Matthew 25:21; Revelation 21). Faith can be seen as one essential step in redemption. A question some carers ask is:

Are there any steps in redemption that are beyond someone with dementia?

Some theologians seek to list and then order the steps in redemption based on passages like John 1:12 and 3:3-5 and Romans 8:30. For example, Murray suggests *predestination, calling, regeneration, conversion/repentance/faith, justification, adoption, sanctification, perseverance,* and finally *glorification.*[1]

---

1 John Murray, *Redemption Accomplished and Applied* (London: Banner of Truth, 1961),

This method is problematic, as there are arguments over what each step means and there are areas of overlap. However, it provides a useful list of steps to see if any is potentially beyond someone with dementia.

Most appear to be exclusively acts of God, e.g. predestination, calling, regeneration, conversion, justification, adoption, and glorification.

Some may question *calling*, on the basis that God may *call* but a person with dementia may not *hear*. However, this relies on a too literal and cognitive understanding of *hear* and a diminished sense of the power of God. To think that God could call and not be heard makes no sense of a God who is all powerful and all good. It is also contrary to the evidence in chapter 2. *Sanctification* is primarily a once off act of God, but also an ongoing process.[2] However, both are divine acts. God is the only source of true holiness in people. As an ongoing process (e.g. Hebrews 12:14), there is an aspect of living out that new status, but it is done through word and Spirit, not essentially by human effort.[3] The ongoing work of Christ and God's work in perseverance (discussed below) may assist. Thus *sanctification* does not appear to be beyond someone who experiences the other 'steps'.

So the particular 'steps' I will consider are *repentance*, *faith* and *perseverance*, as, although they are ultimately the work of God, they involve some action or response from us.

What does it mean to have faith?

'To have faith' has two primary meanings. It is to consider something to be true, and therefore be worthy of trust.

97-105.

2 See David Gilbert Peterson, *Possessed by God: A New Testament theology of sanctification and holiness* (Leicester, England: Apollos, 1995), 27-33.

3 Peterson, *Possessed*, 73.

It is not enough to believe something to be true if that belief does not result in trust. It is not enough to believe there is God, if I do not trust him to be Lord and king in all he does, including in my life (James 1:22; 2:14-26). *Faith* is not the same as *articulate* knowledge.

Leon Morris points us to Psalm 37.3: 'Trust in the Lord and do good...Take delight in the Lord'. From this he suggests faith is basically a right attitude towards God.[4] It is related to words like 'believe', 'trust' and 'hope'. Believers are united in Christ by the work of the Spirit, and this union is more than propositional knowledge. Morris affirms there is an intellectual component to faith, but faith is fundamentally trusting a person, the person of Christ Jesus.[5] That intellectual component may be known *tacitly*.

James K. A. Smith takes this further. He suggests that beliefs 'are more "basic" than ideas'. We are essentially 'religious creatures' who are defined 'not by what we think—not the set of ideas we assent to—but rather what we *believe*, the commitments and trusts that orient our being-in-the-world.'[6]

Words can still trigger and shape these beliefs, this *tacit* knowledge of God, although for some this may be enhanced by social engagement, liturgy, pictures, music and drama. Smith argues this is how young children and mentally challenged adults come to belief.

Are God's words still important?
Most certainly 'yes!'

However, care is required. We can overstate the need to

---

4 Leon M. Morris, 'Faith', pp.357-360, in J. D. Douglas and others, eds., *The New Bible Dictionary* (Nottingham: IVP, 1996), 357.
5 Morris, 'Faith', 358.
6 James K. A. Smith, *Desiring*, 43.

understand all words or to express agreement in specific ways. We saw in chapter 4 that tests for *personhood* based on cognition are both fraught with difficulty and unbiblical. Such views are properly called 'hyper-cognition'.[7] We can affirm that words shape our relationship with God. Yet this is not 'hyper-cognition'. Words convey God's offer of love and forgiveness to enable conversion. But we need not mandate particular responses, or expressions of faith, from a person converted in dementia. We may simply look for signs of *tacit knowledge*, but ultimately we must leave it to God.

We should not downplay the importance of words. A number of the stories in chapter 2 rely upon the use of words in Bible readings, simple statements of comforting truths, prayer, repetition in liturgical services, and hymns and songs. People who lead services for people with dementia are right to believe that their verbal transmission of the gospel can be used by the Spirit to effect salvation.

When a person with dementia hears God's words (through a Bible reading, sermon, prayer, Bible story, hymn or other format) the Word is still heard. Levels of understanding may vary, but will often include a sense that God is good and cares for his people. Words give carers an indication as to better and worse ways to elicit faith for the person with dementia.

True words can embed *tacit* knowledge and elicit attitudes of faith and obedience that the hearer cannot easily articulate. Many people who stress cognition would not push the emphasis on words into a 'test' that one must be able to repeat theological truths in words to be saved. Jesus did not expect such a behaviour from people before

---

[7] For a criticism of overly cognitivist views of humanity see James K. A. Smith, *Who's Afraid of Postmodernism? Taking Derrida, Lyotard, and Foucault to Church* (Grand Rapids: Baker Academic, 2006), 140-41.

he treated them as saved, as we saw in his healing of the demon possessed man. Thus we should not let 'hyper-cognition' shape our understanding of justification by faith.

Are we changing the doctrine of justification by faith?

I think not. The doctrine, as traditionally expressed, deals with people who have reasonably full cognitive powers, and there is no suggestion that someone with such cognition could have faith other than coming to know the salvation that is in Jesus in the ways understood since biblical times. Rather, we are exploring whether the Spirit may lead a person with dementia to faith in ways that are better suited to his/her situation when the capacity of cognition may be impaired. Our doctrine on the sinfulness of all humanity means that no person can claim to be cognitively able to come to faith apart from the transforming power of God

What does *faith* look like when control of thought and speech are diminished?

When Jesus saw faith in a person he already knew a lot more about the person than we may ever know (e.g. the 'marital' life of the woman at the well: John 4:16-18). Similarly, the style of storytelling in the gospels is very concise, and acts that are recounted may have been accompanied by words that are not recounted.

However, we see in the Gospels a number of instances where *faith* is evidenced by acts. The friends who brought the paralytic to Jesus, and, by implication, the paralytic (Matthew 9:1-3: Mark: 2:4-6) showed dependence on Jesus, and an expectation that Jesus was able and willing to meet their needs. Jesus recognised their attitude as *faith*.

Another striking case is the woman with the discharge,

whose *faith* was evidenced by her touching Jesus' cloak (Matthew 9:22; Mark 5:33-35). Likewise a blind man asked Jesus for sight, and received it (Mark 10:51-52).

We don't know how these people came to *faith*, but we see how it is expressed in simple acts of dependence. *Faith* need not be large or impressive or verbal. It must simply be there, like a mustard seed (Luke 17:6). Such *faith* is uncontaminated by a dependence on law or works. This *faith* may be new and weak (Romans 14) but acceptable to God. It will rely on God's power rather than human wisdom (1 Corinthians 2:5).

How may someone with dementia express faith?

Again I should stress that faith may exist without us seeing it expressed.

However, as we care for a person with dementia, and look for evidence that we are caring as well as we can, we may look for signs of change. In this we can be open to the idea that *faith* for someone with dementia may be awareness of Jesus as Lord, an attitude of dependence, relief, trust, happiness, and the absence of any competitors for the person's affections. We met this in a number of the stories told in chapter 2.

Similarly, words of thanks or an 'Amen' in a service or after a prayer is said may mean a lot more than we think. Relationships and human interaction shape us. When someone does good to us, we say, 'thank you'. When someone speaks to us we listen before we think to listen. When we learn through experience to depend on someone, we may depend before we think about our dependence. *Tacit* dependent thanks to God is not a bad alternative to explicit verbal affirmation of faith, and perhaps it precedes it for all believers.

Carers tell of the privilege of seeing a number of people who lived in dementia specific units with advanced dementia, who struggled to put a coherent sentence together, but whose prayers were majestic and deep.

Should not faith be shown in works?
Yes, the book of James makes this clear. But the Bible does not prescribe the form of works. Someone who needs to be fed, cleaned and moved is obviously limited. There is for some the ministry of example, as evidenced in some of the stories in chapter 2, but even this may be compromised in time.

We should not doubt that someone with dementia can love, if we think of love as being other person centred. A 'thank you' offered in response to kindness, or a smile when prayed for or touched, may well be acts of love. The people who cared for Marg felt loved by her (p.25). As *faith* is a gift of God bestowed on a human being (Romans 4:16; Ephesians 2:8), and we know that someone with dementia is a human being, it follows that a person with dementia can receive that gift. When *faith* is weak, we may pray for God to provide anything that is lacking (1 Thessalonians 3:10). For people whose cognition means they live in the moment we should expect to see 'works' of a moment.

Faith is about a relationship. How can someone with dementia have a relationship with God when they sometimes don't appear to relate to their immediate family or anyone else?
We sense we must have knowledge of a person to have *faith* in that person. Based on the stories I told above, some people with limited apparent cognition appear to come to know and trust God. We can call it *tacit knowledge*, but how

can we account theologically for that, besides relying on our understanding of prayer and grace? One area is our doctrine of the knowledge of God. Various theologians through the ages, including Augustine and Calvin, have noted that some knowledge of God is innate in the human mind:

> *"There is within the human mind, and indeed by natural instinct, an awareness of divinity. This we may take to be beyond controversy. To prevent anyone from taking refuge in the pretence of ignorance, God has himself implanted in all men a certain understanding of his divine majesty."* [8]

God has 'set eternity in the hearts of men, yet they cannot fathom what God has done' (Ecclesiastes 3:10).

I am not saying that *faith* comes from 'natural theology',[9] but that experience of God in dementia may complement the way God has made us. For many people the 'trigger' may be an awareness of needs that humans cannot meet and an encounter with God in or through his word. For others, God may meet their needs that are beyond our knowing.

How does dementia affect the sense that there is a God or divine power?

One consequence of dementia may be the wiping away of one's denial of God, and the creation of a new state in which the truth of God's love may become real, as our natural disposition towards God disentangleds from our selfishness.

---

[8] John Calvin, *Institutes of the Christian Religion* (trans. Ford Lewis Battles, 2 vols., Philadelphia: Westminster Press, 1960), 1.III.1, p.43.

[9] For a reformed summary of the limitations of natural theology see Alvin Plantiga, 'Reason and Belief in God', pp.17-93 in Alvin Plantiga and Nicholas Wolterstorff, eds., *Faith and Rationality: Reason and Belief in God* (Notre Dame, Ind.: Notre Dame Press, 1983), 63-67.

It is hard to know where to take this. We do not have statistics on how many older people come to Christ and how that relates to the number of people who come to Christ in dementia. However, a number of stories I heard are similar in that people who entered dementia with no belief in God gained a heightened sense of dependence and need, and recognised that God could and would meet those needs in ways neither they, nor their carers, could explain.

Surely we have to do something to find God? Isn't that 'something' beyond someone with dementia?
There is a long line of Christian thought that emphasises seeking understanding of God, discovering God and being restless and unsatisfied until God is found.[10] Human initiative does not replace the saving work of the Holy Spirit, but there is a sense that there is some responsibility to enquire. Where does this leave someone with advanced dementia?

Augustine and Calvin were not writing in times that were as 'hyper-cognitive' as our own. 'The mysteries of God' were not for them a sign of theological liberalism. God is ultimately unknowable, but he is approachable, and seeking God has a long biblical tradition (1 Chronicles 28:9; 2 Chronicles 15:2; Psalm 22:26; Proverbs 8:17; Jeremiah 29:13; Isaiah 55:6). Yet when Jesus said, 'Ask and it will be given to you; seek and you will find; knock and the door will be opened to you' (Matthew 7:7), we are not to take it as the only way we may come to know God.

When Paul in Romans 10:20 affirms the words of Isaiah 65:1, 'I was found by those who did not seek me; I revealed myself to those who did not ask for me,' he was talking of

---

10 For example, Augustine of Hippo, *The Confessions* (Peabody, Mass.: Hendrickson, 2004) and Anselm of Canterbury, *Proslogion*, trans. M.J. Charlesworth, in *The Major Works*, ed. Brain Davies and G.R. Evans (New York: Oxford University Press, 1998).

nations, not individuals with dementia. However, we may see that God is not constrained to only one avenue of us coming to know him.

We do not know the full scope of what the Spirit pleads in Romans 8:26-27. However, we may extrapolate from it that the Spirit will plead for our need for salvation when all we know is our dependence and a sense of the goodness of God in Jesus.[11]

Doesn't faith in God include rejecting things that are wrong, like false gods? How does this work for someone with dementia?

Yes, part of being a Christian is having no other gods, and usually this will involve recognising and rejecting false gods. For example, I did not become a Christian until I was 30. My knowledge that my pre-30 thoughts are wrong is necessary to my knowledge that my post-30 thoughts that Jesus is Lord is right. Yet someone who has no access to their pre-dementia lack of *faith* may need only a simple *faith*, without the cancelling knowledge that I require. We can trust that that simple *faith* will be sufficient on and beyond judgement day (Romans 8:35).

So our doctrine of *faith* is not an insurmountable problem. Although this has only been an outline of the theology of faith, it does not appear that *faith* is beyond someone with dementia. We may now turn to *repentance*.

If someone with dementia can believe, can they truly repent?

Jesus said we must, 'repent and believe' (Mark 1:14-15). We may ask what *repentance* means for someone who appears to neither remember unrepented sins, nor to know the

---

[11] Cf. Swinton, *Dementia*, 222.

difference between right and wrong. Can we do better than ask the rhetorical question, 'would we expect God to exclude someone from salvation because we can't observe a cognitive act of repentance?'. I think we can, in part because repentance is not exclusively an act of cognition.

On the basis that no act of a sinner can make them right with God, we may say that *repentance* is not a cause of salvation, although it is part of God's scheme for salvation. *Repentance* appears to be fundamentally an act or state of mind or heart which names sin as sin. It is a truth statement, and a judgement on sin.

As sin was dealt with on the cross, we may see *repentance* as a means by which the obstacle to right relationship with God (i.e. one's attachment to one's own sin) is dealt with in a way set by God. It typically involves saying 'sorry', turning away from sin and turning to God (Jeremiah 18:8; 26:3; Luke 15:11-24; 18:13; 19:8). However, if someone has no sense of their own sin, no pride in their sin, and no attachment to their own sin, we may ask if there is an obstacle to right relationship with God for a person with dementia who has a simple trust in God. *Repentance* ends with looking to Christ for everything, and this appears to be the case with a number of people whose stories are recounted in chapter 2.

A brief look at the 'tests' in 1 John may help us here. I have argued that there is evidence that people with dementia can, in some ways, come to trust Christ and love others (i.e. the first two tests). Yet John teaches that we still sin. If someone has no cognitive sense of sin, it follows they cannot deliberately 'continue to sin', which is the third of John's tests. For some, they may not remember from moment to moment, so they neither deliberately continue to sin nor are attached to their sin. They may nevertheless still have some *tacit* sense of sin. Either way, they will still experience versions of sin (e.g. moments of selfishness) that need 'an advocate with the Father', which is exactly what John says they will have if they have faith (1 John 2:1; cf. John 14:26). Thus it appears that *repentance* is not an insurmountable obstacle to someone with dementia.

If someone with dementia can believe and repent, can they persevere?

Some may doubt the will and ability of someone with dementia to persevere in the faith. What is here one moment may be gone the next for someone who lives in the present. However, thankfully, it seems that *perseverance* is also an act of God: 'The Lord is faithful. He will establish you and guard you against the evil one' (2 Thessalonians 3:3).

A person whose attitude to God is changed by the Spirit to one of acceptance and dependence will not be let go: 'My sheep hear my voice, and I know them, and they follow me. I give them eternal life, and they will never perish, and no one will snatch them out of my hand' (John 11:27-29). The testimony of Marg taps into this (p.25). Ultimately Jesus not only gives faith but is the perfecter of faith (Hebrews 12:2). This is a great comfort to all, but particularly to carers who look on and wonder what they can do to help the weakest people in their care. We may trust that their prayers may be answered by the perfecter of faith.

There is of course the challenging warning in Hebrews 6:4-8 of Jews who had become Christians going back to Judaism and 'falling away'. Reconciling this passage with the passages of assurance in John and Romans 8 is beyond this book. However, for me, the sense of Hebrews 6 is the choice of sin so overtaking a person that they become lost to God. It is an intentional rejection of God, which does not appear to accord with the struggles a person with dementia appears to experience as they seek to access their memories.

What about anti-social behaviour and 'sin' in dementia?

One aspect of the 'middle' stage of dementia that concerns many carers is the anti-social behaviour that can be evident in this stage. This can involve uncharacteristic behaviour such as theft, foul language, violence, harassment and promiscuity. Is this *sin,* or a failure of *perseverance,* and does it preclude saving faith?

Some have argued dementia in these cases rips away the veneer of polite social behaviour, and reveals the true, selfish, animalistic person. One response to this would be to say that such arguments appear to be based on misanthropy. However, some may raise similar arguments based on the Christian conviction that our hearts are deceitful (Jeremiah 17:19; 1 John 1:8). Perhaps people with dementia have an outward honesty about the state of their 'heart' in comparison to the rest of us. In God's grace they have an advocate with the Father.

However, as self-awareness and insight are often significantly compromised for people with dementia, we may also need to adjust our expectations, as we do with children.

Does it help to think that 'sins' in dementia are unintentional?

We touched on this above when considering people 'deliberately continuing to sin'. I mention it again because we see, particularly in the Old Testament, that God distinguishes between intentional acts and unintentional acts (Leviticus 5:14-19, cf. Leviticus 16:15-18). I have heard some carers dismiss some poor behaviour as 'unintentional'. While I sympathise with these carers, who want to see and do the best for the people in their care, even unintentional acts are *sin* requiring remedial action (Numbers 15:25).

In relation to acts committed by a person with dementia we may ask if 'anti-social behaviour' can be called 'unintentional', as it is caused by physical illness rather than the heart. Neither intention nor lack of intention enters into it. This view was held by a number of carers I interviewed. This is understandable, as a person with dementia may not 'intend' some behaviour as antisocial or sinful, due to a lack of awareness or insight. However, to focus on 'intention' may be an unnecessary path, because rightness with God does not pivot on goodness of intention. Further, intentions are too hidden, and rely too much on the privileging of will, to get us far. It may be better to say that this 'anti-social behaviour' looks and feels like *sin*, but we may compassionately accept that their 'self-control' and awareness of others is challenged. They simply need an advocate with the Father, and the grace of ongoing forgiveness.

We do not need to second-guess the behaviour, as we have established they are persons in relationship with God. Their behaviour and the feelings are what they are. If we continue to reinterpret their behaviour through the prism of a narrative of defect (e.g. a lack of intention), then we actually de-personalise them. We should give the final word to the cross. To the extent antisocial behaviour is sin, it was dealt with on the cross, and is not an obstacle to someone who comes to faith. It is not necessarily a failure of *perseverance*.

Is there a time in advanced dementia when we cannot reasonably expect any change in that person's relationship with God?

In assessing this we should not be drawn back into the language of capacity, but may still ask when someone no longer speaks or shows signs of hearing, has forgotten how to swallow, is incontinent and immobile, is there hope? The answer is that God's love and power are always sufficient. They are always a person in the eyes of God, always a person for whom Jesus died and always someone God can love and we should love. In Matthew 25:31-46 Jesus assures his hearers that he is always present in the weak, the vulnerable and the useless. We are called to the highest standards of care. We should love them relationally with all the care we can give them, doing what seems to be good for them, trusting in the God who saves.

Conclusion

Although much more could be said on the gospel truth of salvation by grace through faith, I want to suggest there is nothing in our theology that is an obstacle for us trusting that the Holy Spirit can and does bring people to Christ while they live with dementia. Having come this far, we can now consider how we can let the Holy Spirit work through us to do his wonderful work.

Chapter 6

Christian Care that Supports God's Work of Salvation

Identity

One significant gain of working from God's perspective of humanity and *personhood* is we do not have to worry about losing our *personhood*. There are, however, good reasons to worry about losing our identities. It seems that our identities can be largely shaped by how other people relate to us, and what other people say about us. We can resist this, up to a point, if we think they are wrong. But if someone is always called 'Mum' by her children, she will think of herself as a mother. If someone is usually called 'professor', being a professor will be a more important part of his/her identity than it would if he/she was always addressed by his/her first name. If people say I am clever/kind/rude/selfish or whatever, and do that regularly, that will shape how I think about myself.

If I am used to talking with family and friends, and they stop talking to me, that will have a big impact on my identity. I may lose my identity. We need people to relate to us as people for us to keep thinking of ourselves as people. If people only receive care for their physical needs, they may think of themselves only as recipients of physical care, not as emotional, spiritual beings worthy of love. This is what some call 'malignant positioning'. When Christians and their churches fail to care for people with dementia (including sharing Christ with them), they embark on a form of malignant positioning where they deny the person with dementia the opportunity to form an identity grounded in the love of Christ.

Just imagine for a moment if the people you have known for years disappear from your life. What impact would that have on your sense of self, let alone its impact on your enjoyment of life? That is the experience of many older people. This does not only happen to people with dementia, or people in aged care facilities. Many of us seem to have lost the art of visiting people in their homes.

Many carers have far too many stories of children no longer visiting their parents, friends giving up on people they have known for years, and some people never receiving a visit from anyone. Even if a person is visited twice a week for two hours per visit it is still only four hours of interaction with family/friends per week. This, coupled with the short term memory loss and anxiety levels which are often present, provides a precarious base for maintaining or developing identity forming relationships.

The remedies for this include each one of us continuing to visit people regularly until they die, choosing aged care facilities based on the needs of the person in care (not just cost or proximity to one child), and dropping the excuses. These excuses increase with people who are very old or who have dementia. They include not wanting to upset a person, not going 'because it doesn't seem to do any good', not going because they are not recognised, and not going because conversation is beyond the person in care. We may not see the good we do, but we do not know how well our visit is received. Our presence may provide comfort, even if we do not recognise it. Our prayers may be heard by the person we are praying with, and will certainly be heard and answered by God. I suspect some people stop going because they do not want to be upset, without weighing the cost of their abandonment on their family member or friend.

It can be hard to listen to people we love say things they would not have said before they got dementia. One of my friends visited her mother, who had Alzheimer's disease, at least every week for 9 years. For a couple of those years all she heard was either that her mother had no daughter, or that her daughter was an awful person. Yet my friend kept going because she knew that was the loving thing to do.

So the first thing we can do is visit older people we know or we hear are in need, and be prepared to be kind and patient. When I was on a short term mission in Seychelles I went to a dinner where one of my hosts was accompanied by her husband who had Alzheimer's disease. I sat with him for two hours, and listened to him repeat the same two sentences every minute or two for the full two hours. At the end of the evening he seemed to have had a great night out, and my host had the rare experience of enjoying the other guests without having to care for her husband. It really does not matter how I thought about the evening, because I had showed God's love to this couple and witnessed to that love to the others present. I knew it was an evening well spent.

Major providers of aged care have excellent practical guides for caring for people with dementia.[1] For example, Anglican Retirement Villages in Sydney has developed a dementia friendly service to be used in local churches to provide for people in the community with a dementia diagnosis. Elizabeth MacKinlay's books are also helpful.[2] All the aged care chaplains I spoke to would welcome the

---

1   For example, HammondCare's www.hammond.com.au/LiteratureRetrieve.aspx?ID=87868 and Anglican Retirement Villages' www.arv.org.au/
2   For examples, see the bibliography below.

opportunity to help people provide spiritual care for people with dementia.

Can we really talk of 'evangelism' to people with dementia? Knowing stories of people who have come to Christ in dementia, understanding God's perspective on each person, and having a theology of salvation in dementia mean that we can talk of evangelism for those with dementia. This is evident in the mission of Anglican Retirement Villages in Sydney, which is:

> "to serve and care for older people, responding to their diverse needs. With God's help we will enhance well-being, maintain dignity, foster choice and encourage relationships **as we present the good news of Jesus**" [3]

A number of the chaplains I consulted hold that they have a biblical duty and authority to proclaim the gospel to the people in their care, while recognising the wishes, vulnerability and special needs of those people. Some may question the use of the word 'duty', while agreeing that one way to respond to Jesus' command to love our neighbours is to share the love of Jesus to people in our care. This focus on sharing the gospel fits well with research conducted and considered by Elizabeth MacKinlay. She says that people in old age sometimes desire to discuss deeper things.[4] This

---

3 Taken from the website of Anglican Retirement Villages: http://www.arv.org.au/article/22/a-new-vision-mission-and-values-statement, accessed on 14/10/2013 (emphasis added). The blending of Christian care and outreach is also evident in the philosophy of HammondCare which is expressed to be 'consistently evangelistic': see http://www.hammond.com.au/about/philosophy accessed 14/10/2013. See also Meredith Lake's assessment of the mission of HammondCare as 'unapologetically Christian': *Faith in Action: HammondCare* (Sydney: UNSW Press, 2013), 218.
4 *The Spiritual Dimension of Ageing*, 18. See also the studies referred to in Schultz, *Forgetting,*

also accords with my own experience.

I recently visited a very dear uncle in England. He has been a life-long atheist. He dismissed the faith of the congregationalist ministers in our family, and told me I was 'mad' to give up a good job to go into paid ministry. In the last year he had a series of strokes and now has vascular dementia. When we met conversation was not easy because he had difficulty remembering what he was taking about. He spoke for about two hours, and wandered all over the place. At one stage his conversation turned to his death in a way that, for the first time, seemed significant to him. In the past he had said that death was only a complete end to everything. I now asked him if he thought there may be anything after death. He replied, as if he had been thinking about it quite a lot, 'maybe there is, maybe there is'. As I left him I said I would pray for him, and he said, in a friendly manner, 'thank you, you do that'. May God answer those prayers.

While MacKinlay observes, in many places, nurses and pastors are not trained to meet the spiritual needs of older people,[5] the specialist pastors and chaplains I met impressed me, although a number expressed a need for more specialised research, training and resources (for example, visual aids and aged care appropriate Bibles).

Is special training required?
When we recognise that most older people receive care in their homes, including many people living with dementia, it is not hard to conclude that many people with dementia

---

30.

5 For Australian studies on the lack of training for pastors who have responsibility for the aged, see Schultz, *Forgetting*, 36. The lack of training of pastors was not evident in the interviews I conducted, although a lack of 'dementia specific' resources was evident.

receive care from people who are working it out as they go. My lectures on 'Ministry with Seniors' attract many people who want to help seniors, particularly people with dementia, but feel ill-prepared by a life of church attendance.

A number of my students, and chaplains in aged care facilities, have said that it would be helpful if parish ministers were trained so they can give hope to people whose parents and older friends enter dementia without a saving faith. The training should start in our Bible colleges and seminaries, extend into post-ordination training, and continue when pastors are themselves seniors, and have the opportunity to minister to their age cohort. Our ministers also need to see that work with people with dementia is not just a way of expressing love through care and respect, but a context for effective evangelism.

Do we really want to use the 'evangelism' word?
'Evangelism' is an emotive term, particularly when mixed with the very high duty of care owed to vulnerable people. There is a risk that secular commentators will pick up on it and portray aged care facilities, pastors and carers as fanatics trying to notch up conversions even among the most vulnerable. This would be counterproductive and deeply unfair. Gently, patiently being prepared to engage people with conversation about things that matter to them, is a long way from what some people condemn as proselytising. All the facilities and carers I spoke with made it clear they are very aware of the vulnerability of the people in their care, and never do anything against the wishes of those people or their guardians. One carer I spoke with said she believes families entrust their parents to her, and she must respect that trust.

For me, Anglican Retirement Villages in Sydney hits the right note when it includes in its mission, 'presenting the good news of Jesus'.

What should we do when non-Christian children try to stop their parent in a facility from attending chapel or discussing religious subjects?

This can happen for a number of reasons, including a fear that the parent may be upset, or forced, or simply because the children do not want their parent to acquire beliefs that differ from their own. Where the children have power over these matters, the chaplains I spoke with said they respected the wishes of the children, but would still care and pray for the parent.

Won't the binary nature of salvation/damnation scare or upset vulnerable people who can't handle these challenges?

We know God as the God who loves, but he is also a God of awesome power. He is a God who judges and is someone to be feared (e.g. Psalm 111:10; Acts 9:31 and 10:35). Meeting this God while experiencing dementia, particularly if the symptoms include anger, anxiety and fits, may increase fear and anxiety. Therefore, great care needs to be taken. However, Christians will hold that there is something worse than dementia, and that is meeting death without Christ (Matthew 25:1-13). Thus, protecting people from all dangers can be taken too far. Stephen Post criticises care that, 'protects from all risks while ignoring capacities to make choices and live actively, so ...[people]...are to a degree made to be more demented than they are.'[6] There

---

6 Post, *Moral*, 14.

is usually a place for a gentle and timely presentation of the love of Jesus.

People with dementia are not to be pacified and only kept comfortable, but can thrive when they meet the word of God and the person of Jesus.

If we speak of the love of Jesus, won't they just forget?
An issue that Christians with dementia often find deeply disturbing is the fear of forgetting who Jesus is, or forgetting familiar verses, prayers or other words of devotion. While the work of Swinton provides a sound basis for believing that God will remember his children even when they can no longer remember him, the potential for heightened anxiety is perhaps even greater with someone who meets Jesus for the first time in dementia and fears they may forget him before they really know him. The carer may not want to upset the person, and yet the person may sense they need to grasp onto something that seems important but which their failing memory makes elusive.

Experienced carers, particularly chaplains in aged care facilities, recognise this challenge and respond to it with the types of services, Bible studies and personal care described in chapter 1. Repeated experience builds tacit knowledge. They can also be reminded that the God of grace and love, who sent his Son to save the lost, provides the Spirit who speaks when they can no longer speak (Romans: 8:26), and always meets their relational needs with the Father (Hebrews 7:27).

What outside pressures restrict this work?
Much is written on the way we have banished death from our social discourse. Because of improved medical services, the control of epidemics, more reliable supplies of food

and energy and the abatement of wars, at least in the West, untimely death is less prevalent. So we don't talk about it, and many people enter old age unprepared for death. At the time when people most need to understand death, we run the risk of denying them access to a means of doing that by limiting the activities of pastors. There is a serious risk that, as aged care facilities are further regulated and become more dependent on Government funding, the role of chaplains and Christian carers will become more circumscribed.[7] The tactics for dealing with this threat are beyond the scope of this book, but the threat should be recognised within the broader Christian community.

What can we do?
I have three suggestions:

First, evangelicals rightly emphasise the Word in how we know God, and how he reveals himself to us. This applies also with people with dementia. The Word of God is explicit in Bible readings (see the story of Peter above, p.25), and implicit in hymns, songs, liturgy and prayer. The Word of God may need to be used more carefully and sparingly, and supplemented with dramatisation, pictures and music, but it still lies at the heart of how God speaks. Therefore, Christian carers of people with dementia need to be well equipped to interpret and use the Bible in the care they provide. As I said earlier, good pastoral care comes from good theology, and good theology comes from a working knowledge of the Bible.

Second, more work needs to be done, building on the work of John Swinton, Stephen Post, Tom Kitwood, James

---

[7] In a number of my interviews I was assured that no government funding is used for Christian pastoral care, and this work is privately funded.

Smith and others, to work out how to 'get into the worlds' of people with dementia. I am conscious that I have not really done that here. Because of my limited focus, I have not tried to walk in the shoes of someone living with dementia. Carers need to do that. An important step is for all to recognise that personhood is God's gift to give and that a person is always 'there'. Our limitations of knowing what a person with dementia comprehends or senses should never determine the respect they are shown. They should never be treated as if they are not there or won't remember.[8]

Third, if you ever have the opportunity to care for someone with dementia, please never give up hope. Our powerful loving God saves to the bitter end. So care for your family and friends who get dementia. Talk with them. Sing to them. Pray for them. Take them to church services. Hold them. Let God's love for them flow through you. God can save to the very last breath.

---

[8] Swinton, *Dementia*, 82, and Kitwood, *Pastoral Care for the Aged*, 38.

Conclusion

Knowing that someone is always a person in the eyes of God, and God saves until the end of life, should encourage us to persevere in our love of people in our care. Someone living with dementia is always our neighbour, always a person and always deserving of our love. This also helps direct our care. Caring well for the physical needs of people with dementia is essential, but we should recognise that their spiritual needs are also great, and we can help them with those needs.

There is nothing in our theology that precludes us from believing that the Holy Spirit does bring people to Christ while they live with dementia, and much that clearly demonstrates that we should expect it. We do not need to adjust the doctrine of justification by faith to accommodate it, but, rather, recognise the biblical truth that faith is relational and that *tacit* knowledge of God can still be a saving faith. It is a gift from God that is not dependent on our capacities or effort. In some respects dementia may even make people more responsive to God's saving work, as 'the lie of independence' is stripped away and replaced with the truth of dependence.

I am aware I have only scratched the surface of the subject. We would benefit from more detailed studies of individuals who come to Christ in dementia, and greater reflection on the challenges they face and the way they may be helped to deal with these challenges. Yet there is great hope.

To conclude, God has his own view on humanity, and it is higher than secular views and much better than we deserve. The God of grace, who, out of his love, gave his only Son that people who are people in his eyes may not perish but have eternal life (John 3:16), knows people in dementia and makes himself known to people in dementia in ways that issue in saving faith. God always knows who we are, and thus our memories, and everything else we need to love and enjoy God, are with God.

How can we put this into words? We can expand Jeremiah 31:33-34 to read as follows (with additions in bold):

> *"I will put my law in their minds,*
> **even if some of their minds do not work as they used to**
> *and write it on their hearts,*
> **where I can see it, even if others can't.**
>
> *I will be their God,*
>   *and they will be my people,*
> **(yes, including those with dementia).**
>
> *No longer will they teach their neighbour,*
>   *or say to one another, 'That person can't "Know the Lord,"* **because they have lost it'**
> *because they will all know me,*
>   *from the [...]* **healthiest to the sickest,"**
> *declares the Lord.*
>
> *"For I will forgive their wickedness*
>   *and will remember their sins no more,*
> **Even if they have forgotten them"**

Acknowledgement and Thanks

I would like to acknowledge the generous assistance of all the Chaplains and carers who helped me with the practical research for this project. I thank God for the love they have poured out to the people in their care in so many different ways, and thank God for using them to draw the lost to him. Particular thanks are due to Anglican Retirement Villages, HammondCare, and Harbison Care.

I thank the Rev Dr Andrew Cameron and the Rev Dr Michael Hill who supervised a research paper I wrote while studying at Moore Theological College, on which this book is based. I benefited greatly from the comments of Ben Boland (of ARV) on a draft of this book. I also thank the people and staff of St Barnabas Anglican Church, Broadway, Sydney, who have taught me so much, not the least of which is that the goodness of God is never exhausted, and he never gives up on us. Finally I would like to thank the editorial board of Mountain Street Media for their support for this book, and their suggested improvements.

Bibliography

Books cited

Anselm of Canterbury, *Proslogion*, trans. M.J. Charlesworth, in *The Major Works*, ed. Brain Davies and G.R. Evans, New York: Oxford University Press, 1998.

Augustine of Hippo, *The Confessions*, Peabody, Mass.: Hendrickson, 2004.

Karl Barth, *Church Dogmatics*, trans. G. W. Bromely and others, Edinburgh: T & T Clark, 1961.

Karl Barth, *Dogmatics in Outline*, London: SCM, 2001.

Berry, Wendell, *The Art of the Commonplace: The Agrarian Essays of Wendell Berry*, Berkeley: Counterpoint Press, 2002.

Brown, Warren S., Nancy Murphy and H. Newton Malony (eds.), *Whatever Happened to the Soul? Scientific and Theoretical Portraits of Human Nature*, Minneapolis: Fortress Press, 1998.

Calvin, John, *Institutes of the Christian Religion*, trans. Ford Lewis Battles, 2 vols., Philadelphia: Westminster Press, 1960.

Cheston, Richard and Michael Bender, *Understanding Dementia: The Man with the Worried Eyes*, London: Jessica Kingsley Publishers, 1999.

Childs, Brevard *Memory and Tradition in Israel*, London: SCM Press, 1962.

Cooper, John W., *Body, Soul, and Life Everlasting: Biblical Anthropology and the Monism-Dualism Debate*, Grand Rapids: Eerdmans, 1989.

Davis, Robert, *My Journey into Alzheimer's Disease: Helpful Insights for Family and Friends*, Wheaton: Tyndale House, 1989.

Hauerwas, Stanley, Carole Bailey Stoneking, Keith G. Meador, and David Cloutier (eds.), *Growing Old in Christ*, Grand Rapids: Eerdmans, 2003.

Hill, Michael, *The Heart of Marriage: Loving Your Wife with a Christian Mind*, Sydney South, NSW: Aquila Press, 2013.

Hoekema, Anthony Andrew, *Created in God's Image*, Grand Rapids: Eerdmans, 1996.

Hoekema, Anthony Andrew, *Saved by Grace*, Grand Rapids: Eerdmans, 1989.

Keck, David, *Forgetting Whose We Are: Alzheimer's Disease and the Love of God*, Nashville, Tenn: Abington Press, 1996.

Kitwood, Tom, *Dementia Reconsidered: The Person Comes First,* Buckingham: Open University Press, 1997.

Lake, Meredith, *Faith in Action: HammondCare,* Sydney: UNSW Press, 2013.

MacKinlay, Elizabeth, *The Spiritual Dimension of Ageing,* London: Jessica Kingsley Publishers, 2001.

MacKinlay, Elizabeth and Corinne Trevitt, *Facilitating Spiritual Reminiscence for People with Dementia: A Learning Guide,* London: Jessica Kingsley Publishers, 2015.

Murray, John, *Redemption Accomplished and Applied,* London: Banner of Truth, 1961.

Peterson, David Gilbert, *Possessed by God: A New Testament theology of sanctification and holiness,* Leicester, England: Apollos, 1995.

Plantiga, Alvin and Nicholas Wolterstorff (eds.), *Faith and Rationality: Reason and Belief in God,* Notre Dame, IND.: Notre Dame Press, 1983.

Polanyi, Michael, *Towards a Post-Critical Philosophy,* London: Routledge, 1998.

Post, Stephen, *The Moral Challenge of Alzheimer's Disease: Ethical Issues from Diagnosis of Dying* (2nd ed.), Baltimore: Johns Hopkins University Press, 2000.

Ricouer, Paul, *Memory, History, Forgetting*, trans. Kathleen Blamey and David Pellauer, Chicago: Chicago University Press, 2004.

Schultz, Noel Clifford, *Forgetting but not Forgotten*, Adelaide: Openbook, 2004.

Smith, James K.A., *Desiring the Kingdom: Worship, Worldview, and Cultural Formation*, Grand Rapids: Baker Academic, 2009.

Smith, James K.A., *Who's Afraid of Postmodernism? Taking Derrida, Lyotard, and Foucault to Church*, Grand Rapids: Baker Academic, 2006.

Singer, Peter, *Practical Ethics*, Cambridge: Cambridge University Press, 1979.

Swinton, John, *Dementia: Living in the Memories of God*, Grand Rapids: Eerdmans, 2012.

Volf, Miroslav, *The End of Memory: Remembering Rightly in a Violent World*, Grand Rapids: Eerdmans, 2006.

Wright, Nicholas Thomas, *Surprised by Hope: Rethinking Heaven, the Resurrection and the Mission of the Church*, New York: Harper Collins, 2008.

Articles cited

Bogdan, Robert and Steven J. Taylor, 'Relationships with Severely Disabled People: The Social Construction of Humanness', *Social Problems* 36, no. 2 (April 1989): 135-48.

Bryden, Christine and Elizabeth MacKinlay, 'Dementia: A Spiritual Journey Towards the Divine: A Personal View of Dementia', *Journal of Religious Gerontology 13*, issue 3 and 4 (2003), 69-75.

Grant, Kenneth A., 'Tacit Knowledge - We Can Still Learn from Polanyi', *The Electronic Journal of Knowledge Management* volume 5 issue 2, pp. 173-180, available online at www.eikm.com.

Harris, John, 'The Concept of Person and the Value of Life', *Kennedy Institute of Ethics Journal* 9, no. 4(1999).

Jones, Susan Pendelton, and L. Gregory Jones, 'Worship, the Eucharist, Baptism and Ageing' pp. 185-201 in Hauerwas, Stanley, Carole Bailey Stoneking, Keith G. Meador, and David Cloutier (eds.), *Growing Old in Christ*, Grand Rapids: Eerdmans, 2003.

London School of Economics, 'Tacit Knowledge: Making it Explicit', 3, published as a working paper at http://www.lse.ac.uk/economicHistory/Research/facts/tacit.pdf.

Macadam, Jackie, 'Interview with Mary Warnock: 'A Duty to Die', *Life and Work*, October 2008, 23-25.

Morris, Leon M., 'Faith', pp.357-360, in *The New Bible Dictionary*, J. D. Douglas and others (eds.), *New Bible Dictionary*, 3rd ed., Nottingham: IVP, 1996.

Swinton, John, 'Being in the Moment: Developing a Contemplative approach to spiritual care with people who have dementia', pp. 175-85, in Albert Jewell ed., *Spirituality and Personhood in Dementia*, Philadelphia: Jessica Kingsley Publishers, 2011.

Swinton, John, 'What the Body Remembers', Australian Broadcasting Corporation, *Religion and Ethics*, accessed at http://www.abc.net.au/religion/articles/2013/06/26/3790480.htm on 23/08/2013.